ON THE GO

To Mum
and Dad
and James.
The original
players!

PENGUIN BOOKS

UK | USA | Canada | Ireland | Australia | India | New Zealand | South Africa

Penguin Books is part of the Penguin Random House group of companies
whose addresses can be found at global.penguinrandomhouse.com.

Penguin
Random House
UK

First published 2022
001

Text and additional photography copyright © Daisy Upton, 2022
Photography copyright © Lol Johnson, 2022
Illustrations copyright © Katie Kirby, 2022
Foam sheets photograph on page 40 © Shutterstock, 2022
Design © Nikki Dupin at Studio Nic&Lou

The salt-dough recipe is reproduced with kind permission of Emma Marshall (@messylittlebugs).
The high-chair games are reproduced with kind permission of Becky Fox (@beckys_treasure_baskets).
The brands mentioned in this book are trade marks belonging to third parties.

The moral right of the author, illustrator and photographer has been asserted

Printed and bound in Italy

The authorized representative in the EEA is Penguin Random House Ireland,
Morrison Chambers, 32 Nassau Street, Dublin D02 YH68

A CIP catalogue record for this book is available from the British Library

ISBN: 978–0–241–48509–5

MIX
Paper from
responsible sources
FSC® C018179

Penguin Random House is committed to a
sustainable future for our business, our readers
and our planet. This book is made from Forest
Stewardship Council® certified paper.

ON THE GO

EASY FIVE-MINUTE GAMES TO ENTERTAIN CHILDREN WHEN YOU'RE OUT AND ABOUT

DAISY UPTON

PENGUIN BOOKS

CONTENTS

INTRODUCTION	1
MEET THE CREW	4
THE (NEW) GOLDEN RULE	8
LET'S GO KIT	11
TAT BAGS	14
FIVE-MINUTE PLAY DOUGH	26
1. OFF WE GO	29
THINGS I LEARNED ON HOLIDAYS	30
PLANES . . .	37
TRAINS . . .	45
. . . AND AUTOMOBILES	47
OUT AND ABOUT NEAR HOME	59
LET'S GO FOR A WALK	61
THEME PARKS	66
2. ON THE GO TOGETHER	69
FRIENDS AND FAMILY GET-TOGETHERS	71
GAMES FOR PARTIES	73

THE HUNGER GAMES 80

INDOOR GAMES 87

OUTDOOR GAMES 105

WATER GAMES FOR HOT DAYS 117

VIDEO–CHAT GAMES 125

3. ON THE GO TO FORMAL OCCASIONS 131

FORMAL OCCASIONS 133

WEDDINGS 134

FUNERALS 137

4. ON THE GO IN TRICKY TIMES 139

TRICKY TIMES 141

MOVING HOUSE 143

MOVING DAY 146

NEW SCHOOL 154

POORLY PARENTS 157

HOSPITAL STAYS 162

5. ON THE GO WITH . . .   167

THE FIVE-MINUTE BOX OF TRICKS   168

CREATIVE PLAY BOX   171

ACTION BOX   177

LET'S LEARN BOX   183

SENSORY BOX FOR LITTLE ONES   189

CHALLENGE BOX FOR OLDER ONES   195

. . . JUST ME   203

. . . A PEN AND PAPER   214

. . . MY PHONE   221

. . . MY WALLET   225

. . . A DICE   228

. . . SERVIETTES AND SUGAR SACHETS
IN A RESTAURANT   231

. . . A BALL   232

STOP, DROP AND PLAY!   235

ACKNOWLEDGEMENTS   241

INDEX   244

Look out for the colours of the side headings! They're there to help you quickly find the section you need as you flick through the book.

INTRODUCTION

Hi there! I would love to introduce you to this book but I must dash. I've got to pack for a holiday, and drop my daughter off at her ballet class, then nip to the supermarket to grab something for dinner (should've meal-planned in advance but, you know . . . life) before picking up my son from his grandparents.

SOUND FAMILIAR?

I joke, of course. I have actually paused my hectic, non-stop, busy schedule to sit down and welcome you properly to what's coming up in these pages.

Life with kids is without doubt always **ON THE GO**! I often feel as if I should replace my sofas, because the amount of time we spend sitting on them and relaxing does not equate to the space they take up in our living room. A wall covered in plastic moulded climbing rocks for my kids to use would feel a lot more like value for money.

My children, Ewan and Florence, are currently five and seven, and constantly moving and playing and chatting. As a result, so am I. It doesn't matter if we are waiting in a doctor's surgery, visiting relatives or enjoying a nice meal out in a local restaurant. There is no 'sit and wait quietly' with little kids. They don't feel the joy of silence with their eyes closed and the sun on their face, or the pleasure of watching a movie with a cheeky snooze in the middle. They want action, fun, noise and someone to entertain them . . . **ALL THE TIME**!

So, *On the Go* is full of ideas for just that: five-minute games I have used to entertain my kids when out and about – on our travels, on holiday, visiting folks and all the little bits in between.

At home we have toys, games and the telly to keep my kids occupied . . . but what do we do when I'm in a cafe with them both and the kitchen is running well behind so there's an hour's wait for our food? How can I entertain them at a wedding when there aren't any other kids or forms of child-friendly entertainment? What can we play when all I have on me is my purse?

The answers to these questions and more are what this book is full of: quick ideas for ways you can travel light and still keep your little ones busy, as well as games for family get-togethers – because when you've got a whole big group of

kids who are all **ON THE GO** it can be mayhem! With just a tiny smidge of organization, a simple game can bring enough entertainment to give us adults the chance to enjoy some peace as we watch from a distance and discuss all the things we wish to keep from little ears. The games I've included aren't only to give you well-deserved moments of parental peace. Some of my favourite memories from my childhood are when we were playing games as a family and I wanted to share those with you too. Silly recently made-up Upton family ones or games passed down through the generations; games I learned on Brownie camp or on school trips; games I played with my mum and dad and grandparents.

I hope you find the following pages helpful to remind you of some games from your own childhood, to add some new ones to your repertoire or to collect your own. I love the idea of you making this your own personal entertainment manual – a book you can pop in your bag knowing you will be covered if you're ever stuck. And, most of all, I hope these suggestions for activities help you and your family share moments of joy, laughter, silliness and fun – because, when you think about it, that's what life is really all about. And these **ON THE GO** years won't last forever, so let's make the most of it while they do.

SAFETY BITS AND BOBS

There are no age ranges in this book but a little something for everyone aged one to 101. And, as always, everything in here can be set up and ready to play within five minutes. As is often the case with my games, there are certain activities (such as those which encourage throwing things or involve scissors, bubble wrap and particularly small toys or items) that require a grown-up's eyes on them when it comes to children. I'm sure you don't need me to remind you just how speedily a toddler can shove something you thought was definitely out of reach up their nose! With that in mind, do take care in choosing the activities best for you and your family, so that everyone can enjoy them safely.

MEET THE CREW

Because so much of this book is about being together with family and friends, I thought I would rope in my own to appear throughout. Let me introduce them all to you . . .

1 Dominic **2** Nadia **3** Felix **4** Ben **5** Danielle **6** Grandad Willie **7** Jeanette **8** Kenny **9** Me (Daisy) **10** Florence **11** Ewan

12 Jennie 13 Cliff 14 Sneha 15 Seni 16 Amelie 17 Nic 18 Grace

1. DOMINIC

Dominic, brother of Danielle (more about her below), is a Liverpool FC fan (I know – it's a shame, isn't it?!). A cloud-computing geek by day and amateur Tour de France wannabe in his spare time, he's forever jealous of his son's hair!

2. NADIA

Nadia is Dominic's wife and I should really have consulted her before even beginning to write my books because she works on TV game shows, which are often like giant, much cooler versions of some of the games we play at home! Doting mummy to Felix, and together they have been five-minute games testers from the very beginning.

3. FELIX (DOMINIC AND NADIA'S SON)

The happiest chappy who, it turns out, is a true pro in front of the camera. Felix has been assigned the title of Director of Superheroes by the family and they all agree he's doing an excellent job of combating all the 'bad guy mischief'!

4. BEN

Ben, Danielle's husband, started his own football school, which Danielle highjacked with her netballing ambitions! A creative soul, Ben also loves to DJ and come up with games for the kids. On the photoshoot day, he could be found entertaining the little ones by letting them fire ping-pong balls at a cup he held in his mouth, much to their sheer delight!

5. DANIELLE (AKA DLC OR AUNTIE D)

I met Danielle playing netball. I trialled for a team on the same day she did and from that day onwards we were fast friends. I was a bridesmaid at her beautiful wedding, and she did a reading at mine. She runs a netball school in Brighton and coaches kids every week to play the very game that brought us together. Also, once she's on the dance floor, it's hard to get her off again!

6. GRANDAD WILLIE

My husband's dad: Scottish and super handy and helpful – most of the shelves in our house have been made and put up by Grandad. He's a prolific sweetie distributor, which is why the kids can often be found hanging from his pockets!

7. JEANETTE (GRANDAD'S WIFE)

Jeanette's profession as a care assistant to the elderly is perfect because she is incredibly kind and patient, which is why the children love playing hide-and-seek and having bedtime snuggles with her. Although she is from Manila in the Philippines, Jeanette loves the cold weather in England.

8, 9, 10, 11. MY HUSBAND KENNY, ME, FLORENCE AND EWAN

My little awesome foursome. Ewan and Flo are now at school and loving it, and me and their dad are enjoying the daily peace that brings us as we work from home! Our favourite place to be is out and about, and we can be found in a playground or park most weekends or, if not, having a kitchen disco.

12. JENNIE (AKA MUM OR NANNA)

My mum: a retired games and PE teacher (now you know where I get it from) and netball and badminton coach. She's incredibly kind and friendly until she's playing a sport and then you'll see she is highly competitive – and has been known to attempt to win by any means possible!

13. CLIFF (AKA DAD OR POPS)

My dad: also retired and once a semi-professional footballer. Equally competitive as my mum, which is why during my childhood my brother and I could often be found spectating as my parents took a match of garden badminton to a tie-break set!

14. SNEHA (AKA AUNTIE SNEHA)

My best friend from school, Sneha and I have stuck together since our formative years right through to our gardening years! She is Ewan's godmother; she shares her love of books, science, nature and Harry Potter with the kids, and because of this they now adore her as much as I do.

15. SENI

I met Seni when we worked together at the FA. On our lunch breaks we would play highly competitive table tennis matches against each other, passing an old trophy back and forth, depending on which team won. Nic, one of my best friends, also started working at the FA, and that's where she and Seni met.

17. NIC (AKA AUNTIE NIC)

I first met Nic playing netball for our county. She didn't like me at first, but I soon won her over! She's Ewan's godmother and one of her daughter's middle name is Daisy. Nic's a fellow founder of Olympic Wall Squash (see page 94) and one of the most optimistic and generous people you could ever hope to meet!

16, 18. AMELIE AND GRACE (NIC AND SENI'S GIRLS)

Amelie is four and loves everything from Spiderman to Elsa. She and Florence are as happy in each other's company as me and her mum are. Grace is one of the smiliest babies you will ever meet, and she loves lobbing a ball around – a future netballer, hopefully!

THE (NEW) GOLDEN RULE

In my previous two books, *Give Me Five* and *Time For School*, I talk about my original golden rule, which is setting up a game and letting the kids find it and decide for themselves whether or not to play. It removes the pressure and makes life easier for everyone.

THIS BOOK IS A LITTLE DIFFERENT.

The **ORIGINAL GOLDEN RULE** is still brilliant if you are trying to encourage little ones (particularly those aged one to five) to play something they might be a little reluctant to try. Games with an educational twist, perhaps, or unfamiliar rules. If you have kids of this age, then some of the set-ups in this book might still be best attempted by following the original golden rule.

However, I have found that as my children have grown older I no longer require the rule, and by and large it's left by the wayside. The brilliance of it is that they have spent so many years being exposed to games and playing them with me (all in five-minute stints!) that they now completely understand that 'Shall we play a game?' means fun! I no longer need to gently encourage them or put them in control in order to help them grasp the concept – they get it!

Obviously there are still times I set things up for them to find for old times' sake, but mostly now I just ask them if they want to do something first. Playing in this way with my children as they have got older has led me to a new rule that I want to share with you:

BEING BORED IS OK.

I know, I know! I have filled all these pages with ideas and tips and tricks to stave off boredom with entertainment. Yes, lovely, wonderful. *But* I don't want anyone, for any reason, thinking they must do these things all the time and keep their kids constantly entertained. No, siree.

If your kids are bored, so be it. Some of the best ideas I've ever had have come from being bored out of my mind. I often found being at home with two small kids exceptionally dull, and so I turned to social media and set up **@fiveminutemum**. And now look! So boredom's no bad thing, if you ask me.

To repeat: kids can and should be bored at times. You don't need to use a game in this book to fill every gap of time. You don't need to always be **ON THE GO** with them. You can play for five minutes, doing something with them that brings great joy and laughter, and then you can say, 'I've got some other things to do now. Why don't you think up something to do by yourself?'

So, that's my current rule. Like everything with kids, each part of life is a new phase where I learn something new and try out different ideas, like trying on clothes and seeing if they fit. Sometimes they do and sometimes they don't. But five minutes is enough. I am **STILL** Five Minute Mum. And that rule never changes.

LET'S GO KIT

So, before we go anywhere, we need to check we are ready. And by ready with kids I obviously mean packing almost everything you own into a small bag! It sometimes feels like that anyway, especially when you first have a baby and need four changes of clothes, twenty-six muslins and a breast pump just to nip to Tesco.

In my previous two books, I have written out a **KIT LIST** and this book is no different. However, this time the kit isn't about equipment required to play all the games in this book; instead it's the crucial stuff I refer to over and over throughout these pages and which works well for me when we are **ON THE GO**! It's the stuff I grab or the things that are always in my bag because I've found over the years I have needed them, occasionally in times of crisis.

AND THEY ARE . . .

1. RUCKSACK

This is crucial because you can have it on your back, while keeping your hands free to grab small children. I used to have an over-the-shoulder nappy bag when Ewan was a baby and it took me **WAAAY** too long to figure out how ridiculously annoying it was before I switched to a rucksack. Two straps only from now on!

2. SMALLER, LIGHTWEIGHT, BREATHABLE ZIP BAGS

I have these in different sizes. They sometimes contain snacks, or changes of clothes or trampoline-park socks. They're great to separate out what you need within a bigger bag.

3. PLASTERS

There's always a boo-boo somewhere round the corner. Scraped knees can often be 'fixed' with a plaster I've found. I also pop some plasters in my purse/ wallet, tucked in with credit cards, in case I don't have my whole bag with me when an accident occurs.

4. WIPES

Of course! The reusable ones are fab; there are loads of small businesses making these now. I find even with a seven-year-old I still need wipes.

5. SMALL QUICK-DRYING CAMPING TOWEL

I often have one of these stashed at the bottom of my rucksack. They fold up really tiny and dry super fast so they are perfect for rainy days with wet children, or if slides, swings or benches need wiping before bottoms are placed on them.

6. TINY BOTTLE OF BUBBLE MIX

Bubbles are entertainment at its smallest and best.

7. LOLLIPOPS

Great for lots of emergencies like feeling travel sick, being bored or soothing upsets.

8. PARACETAMOL (AND A CREME EGG!)

For grown-up emergencies, both my own and my friends'.

9. PEN

It's amazing how often someone needs a pen for something. Have as many pens in your kit as you have kids. Dropping a pen on a National Trust garden treasure hunt does not make for a fun family day out!

10. SPARE KNICKERS AND PANTS FOR THE KIDS AND SOCKS FOR US ALL

How often have you had to buy socks to enter a soft play?! Always annoying, so socks are a constant.

11. HAIR BOBBLES

Essential for those of us with long hair – or to loop-shut your jeans button if pregnant!

12. HAND GEL

Even before the pandemic I kept hand gel with me, because kids are quite disgusting and often we need to give our hands a cursory gelling before touching anything edible during a day out!

ALWAYS SNACKS

Along with all the above, I often have a bag of snacks and a refillable drinks bottle for each child. The bag of snacks, however, becomes a box when we're going on a longer journey.

The boxes I use are plastic bento-style boxes. I got ours from a small business who sent me a play-dough sensory kit and I repurposed the boxes, but loads of similar ones can be found online and I list a few in my shop on the website.

Our snack boxes have been used hundreds of times – for car and train journeys, in the lounge as a 'treat' to have a special tea and watch a movie, or for a plain old picnic. The little movable dividers make it easy to pop in loads of different-sized things and I don't need to wrap anything. They are one of my favourite items to have!

I thought I would share them here to get us going because as you'll spot through these pages I say the words '**SNACK BOXES**' a lot!

Now obviously this is just me and we will all have our own little kit bag full of things, but isn't it nice to be nosy about what other people have got in theirs? I'm constantly picking up tips and ideas from my own friends, so I hope this is like having a peek in a friend's bag!

TAT BAGS

For those of you who have followed me on social media for a while, you will know how heavily I rely on my **TAT BOXES**! These are two shoebox-sized boxes I have had for years (one for each child). Whenever our plastic collection is added to – often from fast-food meals, magazines or party bags – once it's been abandoned after the initial excitement (three minutes tops), I snaffle it away into a **TAT BOX**. These boxes are kept out of reach and sight. I **ONLY** get them out occasionally to buy myself some peace when the kids are too much. I reveal the **TAT BOXES** like magical treasure chests and put them on the floor for the kids to gleefully explore, while I enjoy the tranquillity of their amazement at all the 'new' toys.

So we know about the **BOXES** – but what about the **BAGS**? To make life easier, I do a similar thing with a bag each for taking with us **ON THE GO**. I say 'bag', but actually it's more like a giant mesh pencil case. Florence has a large orange one I got from a supermarket stationery section, and Ewan has a blue version of the same. I mostly use **TAT BAGS** when we are going somewhere where we will sit down to eat – such as a cafe or restaurant – but I also take them anywhere and everywhere I can.

The **TAT BAGS** have changed over the years based on the ages of the kids, what they are into and where we are going. So, for example, I might have one that's been in use for ages to grab when we are popping out to a restaurant, but I will refresh and update it for when we are about to go on holiday. But they are always there, usually sitting somewhere near (what was, and we still call) the nappy bag, which we take out whenever we go somewhere with the kids (even though it's been some time since they required nappies!). The bags live close to where we exit the house, ready at any given moment to come with us and provide moments for me and my husband to glance at each other across a restaurant table, sipping our drinks silently with a look of 'Thank God we brought those with us!' in our eyes.

WHAT'S IN THE BAG?

So, on the following pages are examples of the various **TAT BAGS** I've had over the years. They include plastic **TAT**, yes, but they also contain stuff I've pulled together specifically to entertain the kids at different ages. I probably should have thought of a better name for them really, but who has time to think up funky names for stuff like this? Not me! Feel free to use the following examples as a guide to help you construct your own **TAT BAGS** from whatever you already have around the house, and, if you fancy it, please do **SHOW US YOUR TATS** by tagging your own creations on social media with **#TATBags**.

The bags are often randomly filled. The trick is to put stuff in them that your child already loves playing with, but a smaller version of it. So, for example, if they love Hot Wheels™ tracks, grab one piece of track and a few cars to put in your bag. If they really enjoy playing with their toy kitchen, perhaps grab a cup, a plate, a spoon and a handful of play food.

Regardless of what you grab, though, I tend to make sure every **TAT BAG** contains something for . . .

- **MARK-MAKING** – for example: whiteboard markers, crayons or pencils

- **CONSTRUCTION** – for example: blocks, bricks, magnetic tiles, LEGO® or play dough (homemade recipe on page 27)

- **MOVEMENT** – for example: a ball, mechanical or wind-up toys or vehicles

- **ROLE PLAY** – for example: characters or figures (people or animals)

Flick through the next pages to see the kind of **TAT BAGS** I've made for my kids . . .

AGE 1-2

Here is an example of the sort of things I gathered for a **TAT BAG** when my little ones were around this age. Obviously the key thing here, as we all know, is to not give them anything too small as they are likely to put things in their mouths, so anything with even the slimmest chance of being wedged into an orifice is off the menu! Chunky toys, sensory and tactile items, and things that can be played with multiple ways are best.

A cup can be used to hide things in, balance things on, put things in and out of, as a hill in role play, as a crayon holder, to clip the pegs to . . . The list is endless. So if you're creating your own bag, it doesn't have to be exactly these items, but something similar you have lying around might just buy you that precious five minutes to flick your eyes across a menu in a restaurant in peace!

- some crayons and scrap paper

- 3 small-world figures

- a plastic cup

- 2 pegs

- a DUPLO® car constructed of four bits of DUPLO® and a wheel base

- a book with something movable like flaps that lift up

- a rubber sensory ball

- a thing that lights up and vibrates when you push the button (no, not what you're thinking . . .)

- a twisty thing

- a puppet (we have a rubber shark one that the kids love)

AGE 3-4

Now they are a little older, you can start to add a few creative items into the **TAT BAG**. Things like a pot of play dough or magnets that they can connect together to build things are now an option.

Kiddies this age are still quite dependent on you. I expect you'll still be shifting drinks out the way and removing all metal cutlery from within their reach the second you sit down at a restaurant table, but they're at least able to concentrate for a few minutes playing with **TAT** like this before asking if there is ice cream on the menu! Again, grab any similar items you have to create your own, but try to keep it nice and simple.

- a squeeze ball

- a pot of play dough and 2–5 accessories for shaping it, rolling it, cutting it and so on

- some magnetic tiles and wheels

- some stickers

- a colouring book

- 2 toy vehicles

- some scented fluorescent pens

- a magnifying glass

- a snap band/bracelet

- a pop-it toy

AGE 5-6

I've given two options here because this is the age where I found that the **TAT BAGS** really come into their own. The kids are a bit older and able to keep busy with a bag like this, often for **MORE THAN** five minutes! Yes, I know – it's lovely! They might draw or colour or build independently or with a sibling or friend.

However, they are also likely to get bored of what is in there relatively quickly, so it's worth changing what's in the **TAT BAGS** more regularly. Kids this age don't quite have the magical innocence of a three-year-old who looks at a toy car like it's a miracle; instead they need to get a bit clever about how to play, and that's why it's good to have a couple of options **ON THE GO** at once!

- a fan

- 4 small animals

- a Koosh ball

- a handful of LEGO® including wheels

- a 'paper sword' flicker

- squishy toy characters (we have a couple of well-squished PAW Patrol ones)

- a notebook and pencils

OR . . .

- 5 small-world people

- a small box and tissue (to make a bed)

- a ribbon on a stick

- a book

- a small Slinky-type spring

- some bangles

- a small soft toy

- a colouring book and pencils

- some stickers (I often have half-used sheets of stickers)

AGE 6+

At this age I've found that kids don't tend to need a **TAT BAG** as much to be entertained. They will be able to do the restaurant's own colouring sheet if they have one (all hail Pizza Express!) or have a go at reading the menu or just generally chat. But, if you're after ideas, the **BOX OF TRICKS** or the games in the last chapter, '**On the Go with . . .**', might be useful (starting on page 167).

> You can make your own fidget toys for the bags by filling a deflated balloon. I've used waterbeads, foodstuff like rice, lentils or flour, hair gel or conditioner, leftover play dough (when it goes brown!) and even water in the past! You might need a funnel when putting some of them into the balloon; I use the one that came with my dishwasher to fill it with salt. Then just tie a knot in it and you've got a little tactile toy to keep kids occupied or calm for a while!

If you want to make lots of different colours, just use plain boiling water and then split the dough up into balls and add the food colouring afterwards, kneading it in. You might want to wear rubber or latex gloves to do this, so your hands don't also go rainbow colours!

This recipe is not edible, but it is taste safe, so it's OK if little ones accidentally put it in their mouths.

This will stay soft if it's wrapped in cling film or similar. You can keep it in an airtight container for up to six months.

FIVE-MINUTE PLAY DOUGH

GRAB:

- a regular-sized mug
- a mixing bowl
- a tablespoon

INGREDIENTS

- 1 mug of plain flour
- /12 mug of table salt
- 2 tablespoons of cream of tartar
- 1 tablespoon of grapeseed oil (*any oil will do but grapeseed is odourless*)
- 1 mug of boiling water
- food colouring (*optional*)
- rubber or latex gloves (*optional*)

TO MAKE . . .

1. Tip a full mug of plain flour into the bowl.

2. Refill the same mug to halfway with the table salt and tip it into the bowl. Add the cream of tartar and oil to the mixture and give it all a stir.

3. Fill the mug with boiling water and, if you want to, add a few drops of food colouring of your choice.

4. Mix the whole lot together with the spoon until it forms a ball. Finally, knead the lovely warm dough until it's cool enough to hand to the kiddos.

OFF WE GO

THINGS I LEARNED ON HOLIDAYS
PLANES . . .
TRAINS . . .
. . . AND AUTOMOBILES
OUT AND ABOUT NEAR HOME
LET'S GO FOR A WALK
THEME PARKS

THINGS I LEARNED ON HOLIDAYS

When Ewan, my eldest, was fourteen months old, we moved from a centre-of-town terraced house to a more suburban cul-de-sac. We got very lucky because our new neighbours, Lisa and Colin, were wonderful, and, as parents themselves, full of excellent advice and funny anecdotes.

I remember chatting to Lisa, with a wriggling Ewan in my arms, and asking her if she wouldn't mind watering the plants because we were off on our first family holiday.

She agreed and told me how her boys had always loved going away too. Then she gave me a knowing look and said, 'But for us parents, holidaying is a bit different once you have kids, isn't it . . .? I like to call it **SSDL**.'

I looked at her, puzzled. 'What does **SSDL** mean?'

'**Same Sh*t, Different Location**,' she said.

I laughed at the time, but **BOY** was she right . . .

I vividly remember that first holiday with Ewan – including a 4:30 a.m. wake-up after I had stayed up enjoying the evening until 2:30 a.m. That day, the game was basically to let him crawl over my face as I lay on the tiled floor of a beautiful Spanish villa trying to stop the room spinning! We also missed our flight home because we seemed to still be in couple mode and forgot we had to also pack up for our son, and therefore left ourselves with fifty-five minutes to catch the flight, when the airport was a forty-minute drive away. Nice one! **SSDL** indeed.

As I'm sure you already know, no, it isn't quite the same going on holiday with kids in tow. But that's OK. There are a few things I can suggest that might just make the **SS** a little easier so that you can enjoy the **DL** – even if the **DL**s are only day trips out from your house and a holiday away is just a pipe dream.

(Another thing everyone learns with kids is how rapidly money vanishes – and how expensive it is to go anywhere in the school holidays!)

But first, if you're fortunate enough to get away on a holiday, overleaf is a list of things I wrote after my first trip abroad with two small children. Some stuff I learned the hard way, and others were tips passed on to me, which I gladly implemented.

1. FORGET ABOUT IT

Try not to constantly compare to what holidays **USED** to be like. This won't be the same as your pre-kids trips – days full of tanning, napping, pool dips and drinking till the early hours. **THOSE DAYS ARE GONE!** Let it go and prepare yourself to appreciate holidays in a new (ahem, massively less relaxing) way. There are always the retirement years to look forward to ... right?!

2. WHAT HOLIDAY?

Don't tell the kids about your holiday too early. Counting down seventy-five sleeps ain't no fun. A week before to build excitement is plenty, I find.

3. PACKING CUBES

Neat zippy bags you can buy online are excellent. It means I can sort and pack my kids' stuff easily. Spare plastic or canvas bags would also do the trick but I find having separate bags within the case for swimwear, shoes, nappies, accessories and so on incredibly helpful.

4. TATS AND SNACKS

Don't forget to load up **TAT BAGS** (page 14) and **SNACK BOXES** (page 13). These are crucial. I'd rather forget my own knickers than these lifesavers!

5. SUCK IT UP

If flying, pack some **LOLLIPOPS** for take-off and landing to help little ears. They can suck them slowly, and hopefully the constant swallowing will help relieve the pressure.

6. 100ML OR LESS OF FUN

Despite my doubts, play dough did get through airport security. It sounds a bit bonkers to pack some play dough in your hand luggage but it's worked brilliantly for us. Turn to page 39 to see how we played with it on the plane.

7. THIS JOURNEY WILL END

Kids on any kind of transport are a pain in the backside. They just are. Accept it and repeat the mantra: **THIS JOURNEY WILL END**.

8. THE KIND OF FLOATER WE ALL WANT

A more serious one: take **FLOTATION DEVICES**, because when kids are drowning they are **SILENT**. They don't shout 'Help!' or splash around. Florence has been attending swimming classes since she was ten weeks old, but we had a momentary scare poolside with her on our first holiday, and saw another child in a scary situation too. Don't be fooled – swimming pools are dangerous as well as fun. This also applies to lakes, rivers and the seaside – a little one can swim out of their depth very easily or find the water too cold. After the pool scare, Florence wore a little life jacket for the rest of our trip, so armbands or any other flotation devices are always worth taking up space in your luggage. Also, buy swimwear that shows well underwater so you or a lifeguard can spot your children easily if they do get into difficulties. Bright oranges and reds are best, and try to avoid pale blue or white.

9. SACK OFF THE ROUTINE

Don't try to stick to anything. Eat when you're hungry. Let them sleep whenever they want and stay up past their bedtimes. Screw the screen-time rules. It does absolutely no harm to take a break from routine, and trying desperately to clock-watch when you're away just steals a bit of everybody's freedom. Find a holiday rhythm that works for you. It's a holiday for the whole family, after all.

10. CHIPS, ICE CREAM AND MORE CHIPS

If they're anything like my kids, yours will mostly eat chips and ice cream. I made my peace with that early on!

11. THE NON-ELECTRONIC MEMORY BANK
Take five minutes regularly to just quietly watch them enjoying themselves. Take pictures in your head as well as on your phone.

12. TEAMWORK MAKES THE DREAMWORK
If you can go on holiday with grandparents or friends who will happily take turns watching the kids, I highly recommend it.

13. A CHANGE IS AS GOOD AS A REST
It might be **SSDL** sometimes, but that **DL** can be all you need to really shake yourself up, take stock and re-evaluate things. Like, what fun it is to be away together as a family.

AND ONE JUST FOR YOU:

No one gives a shiz about how you look in your swimming stuff. Look around you at any pool or beach you go to and you will see every kind of titty, overhang, bum crack, wobbly bit, white bits or tanned bits you could ever wish to see. It's glorious. Go and join them. Your holiday is a place to be free, and you flippin' well deserve it.

PLANES . . .

Now one slight advantage of plane travel over cars and buses is that you have a teeny-weeny pull-down table in front of you, which you can use for activities. The disadvantage, of course, is that sometimes the seat-belt light goes *bing-bong* and you have to strap down a toddler. Then it's basically a battle of wills as to who will cry first: kid or parent. I once gave Ewan a single raisin every minute as we were coming in to land at Manchester airport. It was all I had left and made for an incredibly tense twenty minutes as we tried desperately to calculate what would run out first – the box of dried fruit or the kilometres left on the flight path.

I often tried to book flights around nap times in the hope they would sleep for a bit. It occasionally worked. A nap or overnight sleep is the best we can all hope for to make the journey go smoothly, but often that isn't the case and our little ones need to be entertained – or they might resort to just kicking the seat in front, which isn't generally popular! Obviously, once young ones get to a certain age a tablet or an in-flight movie will hold their attention for a decent amount of time, but if you find yourself with a toddler like Florence – who quite literally tested my '**FIVE MINUTES ONLY**' capacity on a flight back from Portugal – you can bet you're gonna need a veritable sleeve-full of sitting-down entertainment ideas. So here are a few on the next pages . . .

A small, thick cardboard tube from foil or cling film makes a good roller for play dough, and you can stick it in the recycling after use.

1. PLAY DOUGH

Yep, I know I said it before, and you may have thought all that social media had finally addled my brain, but a small pot of play dough on a plane has provided me with five minutes' worth of entertainment for a busy toddler countless times. So long as you don't leave your kids totally unattended with it (which you can't anyway!) then playing with play dough and some little accessories can be a great way to keep little hands busy.

I tend to add one small pot to my **TAT BAG** (page 14) along with a couple of cutters, a mini rolling pin and a few accessories like muffin cases, cut-up paper straws or large buttons. A recipe to make your own is on page 27.

- **Cupcakes and ice creams** – shape the play dough into small balls and pop them in the cones or cases, then decorate them with paper straws and buttons. If you don't have cases, the crew might give you some paper cups instead.

- **Make long sausages** and shape them into letters or numbers, or chop them up with the plastic cutlery that comes with any aeroplane food or drink.

- **Spa days** – pretend to have a manicure and make each other long fingernails.

- **Make prints** of things around you by pressing flattened play dough on it – a seat-belt buckle, or a bit of plastic cutlery maybe. Make a print without the other looking and see if they can guess what it is.

- **Crack the egg** –wrap a small toy or item from your **TAT BAG**, or piece of paper with something written on for older ones, in a bit of play dough. Then let your child 'discover' what you've hidden in the egg.

Sometimes entertainment packs for children contain triangular-shaped crayons with flat sides. These are well worth saving as they don't roll off tables, so are ideal for travelling with.

2. FOAM SHAPES

You can buy already-cut little shapes made of thin foam, or alternatively you can buy A4 sheets of the foam and cut out shapes yourself before you travel. Either way, thin craft foam will stick to smooth surfaces using just water, so this is why having a few of these is handy for an aeroplane!

Get out your shapes on to the tray table and then your child can dip their finger into a cup of water and stick the shapes to the windows or tray. They could make pictures or patterns. Alternatively, you could write letters or numbers on the foam too; your child could try to order their name or write a funny message to someone else they are travelling with. Once finished you can easily remove them and wipe away any excess water with a tissue.

3. STORAGE-POUCH WASHING LINE

Usually when you're on a plane you have a storage pouch at knee level, which is attached to the seat in front of you. It will often have the plane safety information and a magazine in it.

If you have a length of ribbon or string with you, you can tie it between two or three of these pouches and make a little washing line. Let your little one peg things to it. You could also write letters on wooden pegs and they could spell words or their name, or peg up their socks or a pack of tissues. Whatever keeps them busy for a minute or two!

4. SNACK OR TOY TOMBOLA

Often planes provide you with a little sick bag for those 'just in case' moments, or if they don't you can ask for one. You can then use these little bags to play with. Perhaps hide toys inside them for tiny ones to discover and put in and out. For older ones perhaps set up a game of Toy Tombola. Rip up five bits of paper and write the numbers 1, 2, 3, 4 and 5 on them, then pop them inside the bag as 'tickets'. Put five toys from your **TAT BAG** out on the tray table in a line. Ask your child to select a 'ticket' from the bag. Whatever number they pull out 'wins' them a toy from the line; count along it to see what they've won. Perhaps do one toy every minute, so they have a minute or so to play with that toy as their prize before they move on to the next one.

an architect . . .

a computer scientist . . .

If you don't have an interactive book, adding Post-its to the pages of any picture book can be a way to make your own.

5. THE ENTERTAINMENT LOOP

Intersperse these games between playing with the **TAT BAG** toys (see pages 14–25), reading a book (ones that have interactive elements such as flaps, hidden items or play value are always a big hit), trips to the toilet (for entertainment walks as much as actually needing to use it), snacks, watching something on an in-flight TV or tablet screen, and swapping seats with a fellow adult you're travelling with. This is all on a continuous loop, only moving on to the next thing when they have really had enough of whatever activity you're currently on, and going back to the first activity when they've exhausted them all (and you!).

Train stations can be busy and confusing, especially for little ones. See pages **58–59** for being with kids in busy places.

TRAINS . . .

Now, as well as playing all the games I've already discussed for planes, here are a few tips from my times travelling on trains with my two since they were babies of six months old, mostly going from Manchester to London.

1 Kids under the age of five travel for free on British trains. **HOWEVER**, good as this sounds, it also means you **CANNOT** reserve a seat for them. So, if like me, you're travelling with a two-year-old and a four-year-old, it's expected that you can all comfortably squeeze on to one seat (or have *both* kids sitting on your lap!), or it's fine for two of you to stand for a two-hour journey. Can you sense my eyes rolling? Obviously you can risk it, and (if you're not travelling at peak times) you can try to find a carriage where all the seats are not reserved and try to grab some together. In this case, I would find someone on the platform as soon as you can and ask which carriage has unreserved seats. Alternatively, buy your children a ticket each (it's usually half the price of an adult one) in order to reserve seats for you all. Yes, I agree: it's a terrible system – free isn't always good.

2 Reserve forward-facing seats for children. Much less chance of travel sickness.

3 Also, reserve or find seats near a toilet, as, if you're a parent travelling alone, you must **ALL** go together, which if it's down a fifty-metre-long carriage can seem like you've been dropped into a *Ninja Warrior* assault course when you have two toddlers in tow.

4 If at all possible, travel over a mealtime and take a 'train picnic' (as I like to call it). Basically, just sandwiches and snacks, but it kills at least twenty minutes getting everything out and eating it. When you're sitting in a fast-moving carriage for several hours, every little helps.

5 A large rucksack! I used to put everything we needed into as big a rucksack I could find to wear on my back. Navigating trains, stairs and platforms with children required both my hands at all times. I also gave the kids a rucksack each to carry their drink bottle and entertainment items.

. . . AND AUTOMOBILES

For the first years of my children's lives, we were based in Manchester while my extended family (two of Ewan and Florence's grandparents and their uncle) lived in Sussex. Because we all like to spend time together, four-hour car journeys were a regular thing for us as we frequently travelled up and down the country in a car for some family time. Six years of completing this journey roughly every six to twelve weeks meant that I clocked up quite a few tips and tricks for helping my little ones cope with car trips from newborn to age seven. They've seen us through traffic jams, travel sickness, boredom and everything in between!

So I have popped down some of my top tips below from those years of jaunting up and down the M6 . . .

TRAVEL AT NIGHT

If at all possible, travel at the kids' bedtime! This is our usual trick. We have something easy like an oven pizza for dinner, which everyone eats on napkins to avoid more washing-up. The kids then go up for a bath and get into PJs before we pack the car. We then hit the road around 6–7 p.m. (bedtime) so the kids sleep for most of the journey. When they were very little, they used to be easily transferred to bed upon arrival without waking, but now they are older they often wake up when we get there and have about half an hour saying 'hi' and exploring the house before a quick story and into bed.

The advantage of this is that us grown-ups can listen to funny podcasts or our own music during the journey; there are no children telling me they are bored or hungry and there are fewer travel-sickness incidents, plus the roads are always much quieter. Win-win! The disadvantage is that sometimes I need to stop at services for the loo and they wake up. It's always a mad dash in and out if we need a pit stop! Obviously, if you're travelling alone with your kids, you **ALL** have to go inside to the loo too – even a sleeping toddler – so a travel potty could be your saviour here!

GET ORGANIZED

If you can't travel at bedtime, organization is my top tip! I always take these ten things in the car with us for long journeys.

1. THE SICK BOX

We have had **A LOT** of epic voms over the years. I now have stuff especially for this kind of scenario. We've spent many an occasion in a service-station car park trying to make six baby wipes clean up nine ounces of milk that has been violently ejected from a toddler!

MY BOX/BAG INCLUDES . . .

- old hand or baby towels and muslins

- a **FULL** pack of biodegradable or reusable baby wipes

- plastic bags to put sick-covered items in

- potty-training absorbent mats (puppy training mats also do the trick and are cheaper!) to sit on after a vom if the car seat is damp

- a spare set of PJs or a onesie for each kid

- a travel potty – this is great for doubling up as a sick bowl, because the liners are removable. However, very little ones don't seem to be able to aim – which is why I always have a towel within reach. The second they go very green or I hear that awful gagging noise, I put the towel over their lap and catch as much as I can. Then I ball it up and chuck it into a plastic bag, which gets tied into a knot to be dealt with upon arrival somewhere with a sink or, hopefully, a washing machine!

Store these items in an old washing-up bowl for super-easy access and to grab in an urgent situation. I first put this together after a one-year-old Ewan ate an incredibly large yoghurt at a Costa Coffee, then decided to return it in kid-from-*The Exorcist* fashion on a very rainy motorway as we travelled north to see family in Scotland. Oh, and did I mention I was eight months pregnant with Florence at the time? So now we have the **SICK BOX**. See what I mean by 'I learned the hard way'?!

2. TRAVEL POTTY

I've included this for its actual intended use. Always handy, and not just for the kids!! (Especially useful if you are the only adult in the car.) Chuck a spare loo roll in the boot with it.

3. SNACK BOX

As I mentioned on page 13, we often take snack boxes in the car. Once my kids were old enough to feed themselves properly, I found it really easy to hand the boxes over to them, and (when the box is closed) the lid creates a little tray too. I let them choose from the box every thirty minutes or so, or I give the boxes to them as a 'car picnic' if we're travelling during mealtimes. It's best to keep the lid shut while they're eating to stop the snacks from going everywhere!

4. SWEET TREATS

Once children are old enough, sweets can be a good way to keep them quiet for a little while, or to stave off car sickness. I sometimes give mine lollipops too, as licking these can take them a little longer. I pick carefully though and choose ones that are flat as opposed to spherical to minimize any choking risk.

5. AUDIOBOOKS

We have a Toniebox, which is brilliant as the kids can change it themselves and pick and choose what stories they like. But you can get other child-friendly audio players or CDs for the car too. Ours loved the *Polar Express* one when we travelled south for Christmas. And audiobooks can also be downloaded to your phone using apps like *Audible* or *Google Play*. There are loads of children's podcasts available for free too, a lot of which are also quite interesting for us grown-ups: National Geographic's *Greeking Out*, The Week's *Mysteries of Science* and Radio 4's *Homeschool History* to name but a few!

6. TAT BAGS

See page 14.

7. MAGIC/MESS-FREE COLOURING BOOKS

These are ace as you only use water so the kids can 'colour' without making a mess. You can buy them from Hobbycraft or from the 'shop' link on my website **fiveminutemum.com** (listed in the 'car journeys' section).

8. TABLETS AND HEADPHONES

If you have these at home, then bring them! If you can, get wireless headphones for children as the absence of wires means one less thing to be concerned about.

9. A CAR BIN (ESSENTIAL)

A bag, a bucket . . . anything will do, but have something dedicated to the rubbish. Tissues, wipes, snack packets . . . It always builds up so rapidly, doesn't it?

10. CHOOSING BOOKS

Books where they have to choose something on each page are brilliant. They can take ages for the kids to go through and they will do it time and time again. Our favourites are again on my website's shop list.

CAR TRAVEL WITH A NEWBORN

It goes without saying that you'll need to stop often when you've got a newborn. The current safety advice (although there's no published evidence as such) is that you should stop at least every **TWO HOURS**. I have seen others advising every hour. This is to allow babies to stretch and move and to reduce the risk of SIDS. If your newborns are anything like Ewan, you'll need to stop every twenty minutes to feed them anyway!

I always travelled in the back of the car with my two when they were tiny so I could get to them easily for soothing, singing, putting a dummy back in or just so they could see my face. If you're unable to do this, you can buy mirrors that can be angled so that you can see your baby from the front seat to check on them as you travel.

Of course it's always best to check the **TRAFFIC** on the routes you're travelling before you leave to avoid any congestion if at all possible. Some of you might well be familiar with (or scarred for life by!) the screams of a newborn who enjoys movement having to endure long stops in a stationary car. So it might be best to try to avoid that three-mile tailback on the M25!

CAR SAFETY BITS AND BOBS

Currently, children are required by law to travel in the correct **CAR SEAT** according to their height and age until they are 135 centimetres tall or twelve years old. It is the driver's responsibility to adhere to that law and to make sure the car seat is fitted correctly as per the riveting instruction manual that comes with it.

There are lots of different car seats to choose from. Some of the websites I list opposite can help with advice on how to find the correct ones for your child and provide clear safety standards to look for on the labels. The main thing is to ensure the car seat is suitable for your child's size and weight; my husband and I set reminders on our phone to review the car seats every three to six months, as kids love to grow rapidly and cost you even more money just when you least expect it!

Babies need to be in a rear-facing car seat and never in the front seat with an active airbag on. In general it is safer for children to travel in the back of a car.

Car seats should also only be used for a journey, so once you have arrived, take your baby or child out of the seat to avoid overheating or other difficulties. Sometimes shops that sell car seats hold events where you can go along for free to find out about child car safety, and many of the shops will check on the fitting of your car seat for you. It's always worth asking if you aren't sure.

For more information on travelling safely with children and babies, you can visit the Royal Society for the Prevention of Accidents website on childcarseats.org.uk, or the NHSUK website or the Lullaby Trust website lullabytrust.org.uk.

The *Waze* app is really helpful when it comes to navigating traffic jams and giving you alternative road options. Also, the *Playground Buddy* app is a favourite of ours to find hidden play areas en route where we can stop off and let the kids burn off some energy. More app recommendations can be found on page 221.

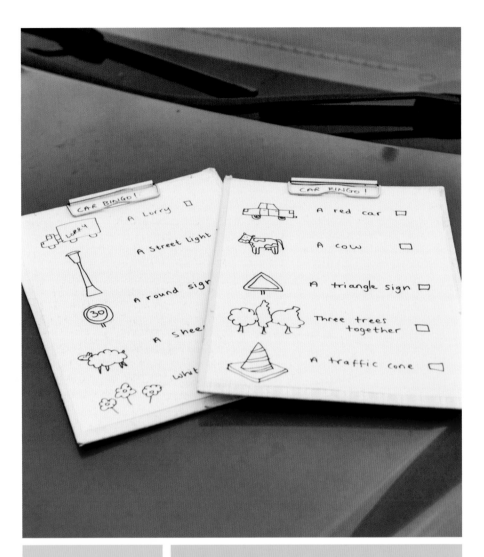

For more games that only require the use of your voice (ideal for playing in the car!), flip to page 203.

GAMES WE PLAY IN THE CAR

1. MAGIC TRAFFIC LIGHTS

Whenever we get to traffic lights, we each take it in turns to make up a magic spell. We see whose spell works to make the light go green! So, as soon as the car stops, I say, 'Iggity zaggety zeem! Make the light go green!' and point my finger at the lights. If the light doesn't go green, one of the kids will immediately jump in to say their spell. Whoever is saying a spell when the light changes has clearly got the right magic!

2. LORRY COUNT

Ideal for a motorway. Everyone chooses a colour. When a lorry of that colour goes past, they add it to their tally. The winner is either the one with the most when the car clock turns to a certain time, or is the first to get to ten or twenty.

3. LINK STORIES

Start off a line from a story. Get your children to come up with the next bit. So: 'One day I went to the park and I saw an **ENORMOUS** . . . Ewan – your go.' They need to be a bit older for this one! I sometimes write down the stories and read them back to them for extra giggles.

4. GUESS THAT SONG

Hum a song and the kids have to guess what it is. Then let them have a go at humming a tune too. Or, if they are much older, beat out the rhythm of the song on a hard surface and see if they can get that.

5. CAR BINGO

Grab a notebook or piece of paper and spend five minutes writing or drawing some things your little ones might see on the journey (depending on their ability to read). Draw tick boxes next to them, and then hand the list to your child – a clipboard or a piece of cardboard with a paperclip also comes in really handy for them to lean on. When they've got them all, they shout **'CAR BINGO!'**

If you're going somewhere busy, grab a quick snapshot of you all when you arrive. Then if anyone does happen to become separated, you have an immediate reference for what they're wearing, to help make reuniting faster!

OUT AND ABOUT NEAR HOME

Now, lots of fun can be had near home without having to fork out for holidays, or deal with all the hassle that travelling with kids can bring. So this section has some ideas for things you can do near home. This can mean in your neighbourhood, or just a short drive away – like a day trip to a theme park or similar. First off, as a responsible mum (ahem!), some notes about safety . . .

OUT AND ABOUT SAFETY

When you're out and about with kids, especially in busy areas, it can feel quite daunting. Here are a few tips to help you feel prepared:

1 Write your mobile number in pen up your child's arm (or buy them a beaded bracelet or similar with your number on it) and tell them what it is. In case they are ever lost, teach them to show this number to any adult who is trying to help them.

2 It sounds silly, but if we are ever going somewhere I know is going to be really busy I put my kids in matching brightly coloured hats or T-shirts. It's much easier to spot them when you're looking for the same bright colour!

3 Regularly point out to them people who can help us. When I enter a theme park, I show my kids what the staff are wearing and how they have lanyards around their neck and say, 'If you ever get lost that is who to look for to ask for help.' Likewise with police officers, train station attendants or people in uniforms. I regularly remind them this is who to look for first.

4 If your child does go missing in a crowd, immediately shout, 'Child missing!' and call out what they are wearing.

5 Teach your child that if they are lost to stand still and only move to ask a person for help (as noted above in point 3) or another grown-up with children. This way you won't all be walking in circles missing each other.

LET'S GO FOR A WALK

If I suggest the idea of a nice country walk to my children (my idea of a perfect Sunday morning), I am met with a response akin to that as if I had suggested we all get together and do my tax return form. Groans, moans and cries of 'I don't want to!' all echo through the house. And yet when we are out there on paths meandering through woodland, kicking stones and finding wildlife, they love it. We often all enjoy ourselves (albeit sometimes with a bit of 'there are sweets in the bag' bribery), and so I have come up with five words that change 'Let's go for a walk' into something they want to do . Here they are:

'LET'S GO ON A HUNT'

Here are five **HUNTS** that we go on:

1. THE CHECKLIST HUNT

I write or draw on a bit of paper about ten things that we might see, such as an orange-coloured leaf, a stick longer than your finger, a pine cone or a puddle, and I pop a little tick box next to each. I also leave about three lines for 'bonus items' they can add themselves. I pop each on a clipboard with a pencil (with a couple of spare pencils in my pocket because they always lose them!).

2. THE COLLECTION HUNT

This requires a bag of some sort – usually a funky-coloured gift bag left over from Christmas or birthdays. Sometimes I make a list of things they have to collect and put in the bag, and other times we just go out with the bag and collect what we see. For littler ones I might give them a big piece of paper with different colours scribbled on it and they have to collect something in each colour.

3. THE TRAFFIC HUNT

Again, grab your trusty clipboards and draw some vehicles down one side of a sheet of paper – perhaps a car, lorry, motorbike, truck and a bus. Then walk to wherever you would like to and find somewhere to sit where you can see traffic from a safe distance. Set a timer on your phone for five or ten minutes, and every time a vehicle goes past put a tally mark next to the correct vehicle.

This is a great way to learn tallying or counting, and you can also predict which vehicle you will see most of. You could also do this with just cars but in different colours. It's also a great way for young ones to learn how many cars are on the roads. Where are they all going?

4. THE RIBBON HUNT

This requires a bit of planning, but is worth it for boring days during school holidays. Grab a long brightly coloured ribbon (or similar) and cut it into ten or so bits. Find the same number of drawing pins as you have bits of ribbon. Now you or another adult goes out for a walk on their own. As you walk, pin a bit of ribbon at intervals on trees or fences or benches. Then go home and repeat the same walk with your little ones and see if they can collect all the ribbons (make sure you also collect all the drawing pins yourself). You might want to draw them a 'map' (rough sketch) of the area with crosses for the ribbons. You could also do this the other way round, with your children and you setting out the ribbons and then perhaps asking a grandparent or some friends to see if they can go and find them all.

5. THE CAR HUNT

Again, this requires a little planning, but it's something we did when we were in the pandemic lockdowns in 2020 to give us a reason for yet **ANOTHER** daily walk, just to get out the house. Without telling the kids, my husband took the car out and parked it somewhere about a mile or so away. He then ran home. (I know! I think he's crackers too!) Later on, when we wanted to go for that walk, he did a brilliant 'Where's our car gone?' routine to the kids, and then pretended to get a text from the car with 'tracker info' and explained we had to go out and search for the clues to find it. The kids very quickly got on their shoes and grabbed clipboards, pencils and paper. I asked them to draw a picture of the car and write down the number plate to look for, while I gathered drinks and snacks. Then we went out. Every so often my husband would glance up ahead and spot an obvious feature, then pretend to get a text on his phone from the 'tracker' and say things like: 'It says to look for a lamp post with a sticker on it' and the kids would then excitedly find it and write it down on their clipboard. Or, in Florence's case, draw a little squiggle! When we eventually located the car, they were so happy, and we all climbed in and drove home.

TOP TIP FOR GETTING INTO CARS AFTER MUDDY WALKS:

Have a very large Bag for Life-style bag in the boot of your car – ALWAYS. Ideally those big blue IKEA bags, as these are the best for this. When you return to your car with your muddy child, stand them in the bag and strip them into it. So boots, waterproofs and wet clothes all go directly into the bag. Then you can pick them up out of it, and give them a onesie to pop on in the car while you pick up the bag of stuff to put into the boot, ready to go directly into the washing machine when you get home.

OTHER WAYS TO ENCOURAGE WALKS

- **GEOCACHING OR POKÉMON CACHING** – you can download apps so that you walk to find things – essentially treasure hunting but using your phone. If you go to geocaching.com there's a video that explains it better than I can and you can create an account and get started. *Pokémon GO* is a similar concept, but instead of finding 'cache' you find and collect Pokémon, which you can see on your phone.

- **COMPASS** – buy a compass (or use a compass app on your phone) and get your little one to give you directions or tell you which way you're going.

- **BINOCULARS** – take a set with you and look into the habitats around you to see what you can find.

- ***WE'RE GOING ON A BEAR HUNT*** – read this book by Michael Rosen and Helen Oxenbury before you go out and see if you can find the swishy swashy grass, oozy mud and other things in the story while on your 'adventure'. Of course, there are lots of other adventure books too.

- ***50 FANTASTIC IDEAS FOR FOREST SCHOOL*** – this book by Jamie Victoria Barnes was recommended to me, and is fantastic. It's filled with lots of ways to have fun in the woodlands that might encourage your little ones to want to go out on an adventure.

THEME PARKS

We are theme-park lovers in our family. We really enjoy rides and noisy days out with the smell of doughnuts in the air. We like fast rides and queuing (joking – we don't like it, but obviously it's expected!) and being fleeced of all our cash (also expected!). I understand they aren't for everyone, and it's also tricky to decide when your children might be ready for a theme park or similar. It is, of course, a personal choice, but when ours were very little (I think aged three and one) we took them to CBeebies Land at Alton Towers to test the waters. We enjoyed it so much we've been back since and to others, such as LEGOLAND®, Gulliver's World and Drayton Manor and always had a brilliant and exhausting day.

Here are my tips for theme-park fun:

1. TAKE YOUR OWN FOOD
Theme-park food is crazy money and also means more queuing, so take a picnic in a rucksack. This also means you can eat said food while in a queue, which means you're doing two things at once and can keep the kids quiet for a little bit with a sandwich as you shift a metre or so every thirty seconds.

2. PLAY GAMES IN THE QUEUE
Games like Simon Says, I Spy, I Went to the Shops (see page 203) and Link Stories (see page 57) all work in queues. You can also invent your own theme-park rides, play Would You Rather? (examples on pages 204–205), and do things like rate the rides they've been on so far in a best to worst list.

3. DON'T EXPECT TO STAY ALL DAY
Go early – as soon as it opens ideally – and be prepared to leave once you've had enough, or go later and stay until it shuts. It's better to go home on a high than keep trooping around with everyone getting very ratty.

4. THINK ABOUT HIRING A BUGGY
You can often hire buggies at theme parks – check before you go. We've done this a few times and felt it was worth it. When Ewan was a bit older and we

didn't have a double buggy any more, we hired a double one at the entrance and it saved his legs on those long walks between rides, which helped in the long run, especially at the end of the day. He and Florence also once both had a quick power nap in one, and my mum watched them while me and my husband dashed off to go on a big roller coaster! Winner!

5. LOOK AT HOTEL DEALS

We've sometimes taken advantage of deals that allow you to stay in hotels overnight and have two days at the theme park included as part of the package. This means you can take it steady with all the things to do and not rush. If your kids are not yet in school, then take advantage of deals that you can find in term times.

ON THE GO TOGETHER

FRIENDS AND FAMILY
GET-TOGETHERS

GAMES FOR PARTIES

THE HUNGER GAMES

INDOOR GAMES

OUTDOOR GAMES

WATER GAMES FOR HOT DAYS

VIDEO-CHAT GAMES

FRIENDS AND FAMILY GET-TOGETHERS

Now that I'm a parent, one of my favourite sounds in the world is hearing our friends and extended family playing with the kids and everyone laughing together. It doesn't matter if I am joining in, or just overhearing the fun from the kitchen – the noise imprints joyous memories on to my soul.

There are points throughout the year when loved ones – both near and far – might naturally gravitate towards each other: Christmas, Diwali, Eid, Hanukkah, Easter, Lunar New Year and other religious or cultural celebrations, as well as birthday parties, Mother's Day and Father's Day and the like. I personally use any reason I possibly can to gather us all together. Pancake Day? Yep, that's a holiday – come on over, family *and* friends!

But sometimes, when there are a lot of people, it can be tricky to keep all the kids busy, and you might perhaps want to play a game to entertain them for a bit and stop any squabbles that occasionally arise from such a rabble of young folks. So I've decided to pull together a chapter of family games, perfect for celebrations or get-togethers. They aren't all my own inventions. There are some old classics in here too – but these are the ones we've played over the years. I hope that by bringing them together into a chapter of this book I can make many more deposits in that happy memories bank, simply by flicking through these pages and reminding myself of these firm favourites.

Another game we play with balloons at home is just us putting a laundry basket in the middle of the room and each sitting around it (usually on the sofas!) taking it in turns to throw or bat our balloon into the basket. First to get it in wins, or first to five basket shots wins, depending on how much time we have!

Sometimes if it's just me and my two kids playing musical balloons, we play the final bit at home without the music. You just have to keep swapping balloons and catching the other before it hits the ground!

GAMES FOR PARTIES

Aside from the usual pass the parcel, musical bumps/statues and pin the tail on the donkey (which are all brilliant games), there might be times when you have a group of children to entertain and you want to trump all the other parents by organizing the **BEST PARTY EVER**! I jest, of course, but when you're at your seventeenth birthday party of the year in a dusty leisure centre, something a bit different is always very welcome. And everyone knows the best way to win the **BEST PARTY EVER AWARD** (as far as the adults are concerned anyway) is to serve caffeine and/or alcoholic beverages. But let's focus here on party games for the young ones! We sometimes blow up lots of (biodegradable) balloons as decoration, and here are two fun games to get rid of them afterwards, so you can pop them in the compost bin.

DROP AND POP

1. Firstly, check that everyone is up for playing a noisy game. Everyone gathers up the same number of balloons.

2. Shout, 'Ready, steady, go!' and players have to pop their balloons with any part of their body except their hands and feet.

3. First to pop all their balloons wins!

MUSICAL BALLOONS

1. Everyone has a balloon except one person.

2. When the music starts, everyone moves around, carrying their balloon.

3. When the music stops, everyone must throw their balloon into the air.

4. Everyone must now catch or collect another balloon. The person without a balloon at the end is out and the music starts again.

5. When you are down to the last two players, they must each have a balloon, and when the music stops they must both release the balloon they are holding and catch the balloon of their opponent before it hits the floor. If they are unable to get it in time, the other person wins.

BALLOON RELAY

This is good for a large group of people.

1. Get everyone who wants to play in two lines (standing as if they were queuing for something). Ideally each line should have the same number of people. Each line has a balloon at the starting end.

2. After you say 'Ready, steady, go!', the players have to pass the balloon to each other in one of the ways below. When the person at the back gets the balloon, they must run to the front of the line and it gets passed back again. Repeat until the person who was originally at the front returns to the front of the line with it and shouts, '**WINNERS!**' The winning team is the first to do this.

WAYS TO PASS THE BALLOON:

- over the top of your head
- between your legs
- alternating between over your head, then under the next person's legs
- by grasping it between your knees
- make the balloons quite small, and pass by grasping it under your chin (no hands!)

What must I look like?!

TIGHTS RELAY

Another version of a relay race but this time with hosiery.

GRAB:

- 2 pairs of tights (use kids' tights for younger ones to make sure the tights don't cover their face)
- 2 tennis balls (or similar weighted items)
- 6 plastic or paper cups (or just have 1 cup if you're playing with little ones)

TO SET UP . . .

1. Divide everyone into two teams.

2. Put one tennis ball in one of the toes of each pair of tights. Give each team one pair.

3. At one end of the playing area, place the cups, upside down, in a line for each team.

TO PLAY . . .

1. After 'Ready, steady, go!' each team member takes it turn to put the tights on the top of their head and knock over the cups by swinging the ball in the tights and hitting the cups. Once all five are down, the player has to stand the cups back up and pass the tights to the next team member.

2. The winner is the first team in which all members have completed the knockdown, and they have to shout, '**WINNERS!**'

If you're worried about sharing soggy saliva-covered boxes, get a box for each person. Just make sure the boxes are the same height for each round.

CEREAL BOX GAME

1. Get an empty cereal box, or any lightweight, tall cardboard box, and stand it upright. Everyone playing stands in a circle round it.

2. Take it in turns to pick up the cardboard box with your teeth only. You cannot touch the box or floor with your hands or knees. If it's too tricky for little ones, let them have one hand or knee touching the floor.

3. Once everyone has achieved this, tear a strip about an inch (two to three centimetres) off the top of the box. Now you all attempt to pick it up again.

4. Anyone who can't do it is out.

5. Keep tearing off strips. As the box gets smaller, it gets much harder.

6. The winner is the last person who can manage to pick the box up at its smallest size.

BINGO LIMBO

Obviously you can play limbo the usual way, gradually making the bar go lower and lower. But if the same people always win, why not mix it up a bit with some bingo and see what happens then . . . ?!

GRAB:

- 10 Post-its (or bits of paper and masking tape)
- a broom or large pole
- a small bowl or container
- pen
- paper
- scissors

TO SET UP . . .

1. Make tickets for numbers 1–10 using the paper, pen and scissors. Fold up each ticket and pop them in the bowl or container.

2. On individual Post-its, write the numbers 1–10. Stick them along the broom/pole in order.

TO PLAY . . .

1. Two adults hold either end of the broom/pole (or balance them on something at the right heights). Hold the end with the number ten quite high so it would be easy for people to reach. The person at the end with the number one holds the pole lower, around waist height.

2. Each player picks a ticket out of the bowl.

3. They must then limbo under the number they got and grab it with their teeth/mouth off the broom as they go. If they succeed, they get another go at picking out another number.

4. You can keep reapplying the numbers and popping the tickets back in the bowl for as long as everyone is enjoying playing. Don't forget to crank up the music too!

THE HUNGER GAMES

And I mean games involving food, rather than somebody volunteering as Tribute and fighting to the death (depends what mood I'm in . . .). Of course, remember to check for allergies first!

THE CHOCOLATE GAME

This is a game that I remember from Brownies and Girl Guides and you might very well remember too! In fact, I wonder if they still play it?

GRAB:

- a large bar of chocolate that comes in small squares (a big sharing bar of Dairy Milk is perfect)
- a chopping board
- a children's knife and fork
- gloves, hat and scarf
- a dice

TO SET UP . . .

1. The players sit in a circle.

2. In the middle is the (opened) bar of chocolate on the chopping board, with the knife and fork and hat, gloves and scarf nearby.

TO PLAY . . .

1. Someone in the circle rolls the dice. If they get any number between one and five, they just pass the dice on to the person on their left.

2. If they roll a six, they have to get up, and as fast as they can put on the hat, gloves and scarf, then pick up the knife and fork and cut one square of the chocolate bar. If they manage it in time (see step 3), they get to eat that square.

3. Meanwhile the other players in the circle are still rolling the dice. If at any point someone else rolls a six, the person in the middle must give up their attempt for chocolate and hand the clothes and cutlery over to the other player, who can then make their attempt to try to get dressed in the items, then eat some chocolate before the next six is rolled.

4. Sometimes it can get quite chaotic if a few people roll sixes in a row! If you like, you can use two dice and try rolling doubles or saying only a double six counts.

DOUGHNUT LIMBO

I saw this doing the rounds on social media a few years ago and it's been a Halloween favourite ever since.

1. Get some doughnuts with holes in.

2. Make a washing line out of some string. This can be indoors or outdoors.

3. Thread more string through the doughnut holes and tie the doughnuts to the washing line.

4. Tell the kids they can each have a doughnut, but they have to eat them off the doughnut line without touching them with their hands!

CHOPSTICK MALTESERS

1. Put a bowl of Maltesers (or similar round chocolate treats) out on the table.

2. Give each child a pair of chopsticks.

3. They can only eat the ones they manage to get into their mouths using just the chopsticks.

4. Alternatively, if you don't have chopsticks or are worried about them being too pointy for little ones, use large wooden spoons and ask the children to work as a pair to feed them to a friend!

JELLY-BEAN HUNT

This game was played one brilliant night out in Soho after my friend Emma decided on a different sort of office party. Each team of staff had to set up games they liked in different venues. My team did a Crystal Maze-style activity, complete with a gaffer-taped makeshift plastic 'crystal dome'. It was the pub crawl to end all pub crawls.

Here's one of the games we got our colleagues to compete in! It works really well with little ones too.

1. Get a large bowl and tip as many jelly beans as you can of different colours into it.

2. Give each player a pair of socks to wear on their hands, and a small bowl.

3. Assign each player a colour of jelly bean to collect.

4. Set a timer for two minutes and shout, '**GO!**'

5. Once the time is up, everybody counts their jelly beans. Any jelly beans not in the correct colour means one of the jelly beans they won in the correct colour must be put back into the big bowl!

6. If you've got loads of kids, you can let four play at a time and keep swapping over. Of course, they get to eat their winnings!

AFTER EIGHTS GAME

I couldn't forget this old classic. You simply pop an After Eight (or any small, flat lightweight chocolate mint) on your forehead and try to get it into your mouth without touching it. Great for a group, as everyone has a try to see who can do it the fastest. Additional laughs for the chocolate smears down faces after!

On my website's shop there is a list of stuff that I stock up on, as well as a lot of investment toys, which we turn to again and again for indoor fun.

INDOOR GAMES

'Oh look, it's raining again.' Words guaranteed to induce a loud sigh from me, especially if we have a family party planned. When I have the kids at home day-to-day, getting out in the fresh air is not only crucial for our physical health (the ratio of breathable air to farts is 1:5 in my household at times) but also our mental health too because . . . well, it's just nice to get out, innit? But, alas, we live in England and so the great outdoors isn't always that enticing, and often indoor games seem preferable. And if you have all the family coming over, essential if the weather does let you down.

I pull out the craft box or the kinetic sand and play dough when it's just me and the kids over the school holidays, but we often play games together too, and when we do here's what we play time and time again, all of which also work for bigger groups . . .

KITCHEN TENNIS

I recently listened to the legendary tennis coach Judy Murray on Desert Island Discs. On her episode, she mentioned playing tennis in the kitchen with her two sons, Andy and Jamie, when they were young. As we know, they both went on to become tennis champions . . . So, I fancied me a bit of that action, and set this game up in our kitchen for my two. VIP box at Wimbledon, here I come!

GRAB:

- cereal boxes (they don't need to be empty)
- plastic plates
- ping-pong ball

TO SET UP . . .

1. Use the cereal boxes to create a 'net' or barrier across the middle of a room with a hard floor. (We like to play this in the kitchen.)

2. Each player grabs a plate as their racket.

TO PLAY . . .

1. You can play any rules you like! We let each player serve twice from the back of the room and you can score a point at any time, not just if you served. You get a point if your opponent hits the net with the ball or racket, or fails to return the ball to you after it has bounced once.

2. The first to ten points wins – or you can play using a tennis-scoring system, so first set wins.

3. We play off the cupboards and walls, and I allow two bounces if we are playing with younger children. It becomes a bit more like squash than tennis and sometimes all kinds of crazy things happen – like it might bounce into the sink or a cup – but that adds to the fun!

4. For very tiny ones I play with a balloon instead as it's much slower moving, so they can still join in.

PAPER SHUFFLE

To play this you need a hard floor, like tiles or wood/laminate.

GRAB:

- two pieces of A4 paper for each player
- a cushion
- a prize (it could be a teddy, the TV remote, a treat . . . anything!)

TO SET UP . . .

1. Put a prize on the cushion in the centre of the floor.

2. Make each player stand on one piece of paper, with the other piece empty next to it. Both players must be the same distance away from the prize!

TO PLAY . . .

1. After 'Ready steady, go!' each player must move the second piece of paper in front of them – towards the prize – and step on to it.

2. Then repeat with the piece of paper they were on before, using them as alternate stepping stones to try to get to the prize as fast as they can.

3. They must not at any point step on the floor.

4. The first one to grab the prize wins!

You could also play this with balloons if you don't have toilet-roll tubes.

WAFT IT

This is the kind of game that I love most. When I first started Five Minute Mum, it was always a game played in the kitchen using stuff that was knocking around that was the most popular with me and the people I shared it with. It doesn't have to look pretty; in fact it's better if it doesn't. The only rules for this kind of game are that it is **FUN** and that the clean-up takes minutes or, in this case, seconds!

GRAB:

- masking tape
- a paper or plastic plate for each player
- an empty cardboard toilet-roll tube each

TO SET UP . . .

1. Use the masking tape to mark out two lines, one on either side of the room – a kitchen floor is ideal.

2. Hand each player a paper plate and a toilet-roll tube.

3. Let the players design their own tube or write their name on it.

TO PLAY . . .

1. Place your tube in the middle of the room and sit behind one of the masking-tape lines. Your opposition player must do the same.

2. Say, 'Ready, steady, go!'

3. Now use the plate like a fan so the draught it creates makes the tubes roll. You are trying to get your tube to cross your opponent's masking-tape line, while simultaneously stopping them doing the same.

4. The first player to get their tube to cross the line is the winner. Pop the tubes back in the middle and play again.

5. If lots of people want to join in, play in teams, with one team on either side of the masking-tape lines.

OLYMPIC WALL SQUASH

There's a story behind this game and its wacky name. When I was at university, during exam season, me and my best friend Nic would go to each other's rooms for a break. We lived in halls that had long corridors, and during one such break we found ourselves sitting out in the corridor with a tennis ball. We started bouncing it off the walls, playing around, and bit by bit we invented this game. We soon started playing it every couple of hours during our revision breaks until we eventually decided on its name (I cannot remember why we named it this). I even once wrote out the official rules for Nic as a birthday present!

GRAB:

- a tennis ball or similar small bouncy lightweight ball
- masking tape

TO SET UP . . .

1. Find a good clear wall space and use masking tape to mark out a line across it horizontally, around chest height (from a sitting position).

TO PLAY . . .

1. Sit on the floor with your opponent, side by side, about leg length away from the wall (or slightly further back if you want), or your backs to the wall opposite if you're playing in a corridor (as we did originally!).

2. One player serves by throwing the ball in the air and hitting it with their hand. The initial bounce must be above the line on the wall. This is the service line. After that, the ball can hit the wall anywhere in the agreed playing area.

3. You get a point if your opponent:

■ fails to bounce the ball above the line with their initial serve;

■ misses the ball after you've bounced if off the wall;

■ hits the ball with anything other than their hands.

4. You cannot move from your sitting position on the floor, although you can lean and stretch as far as you like, and you can only hit the ball with your hands.

5. Take it in turns to serve. First to ten points wins.

For little kids playing this game, use a balloon as it moves more slowly, but don't allow it to bounce if that is too easy.

We play it without letting the ball touch the floor, but you can tweak the rules if it's easier to allow one bounce on the floor after it's hit the wall.

THE FLOUR GAME

This is a game from my childhood – and perhaps yours? It reminds me of my nan because it was a game we played whenever we got together with her side of the family, the Butlers! A friend of mine has since said she played it as a kid but with a jelly sweet in the middle of the flour. I think, though, if I tried that with my two, they'd instantly lose and forfeit the game just to plunge their head into the flour for a treat! But do whatever version works for you. Here's ours . . .

GRAB:

- a deep bowl (we use a plastic pudding bowl)
- a matchstick
- a tray and/or vinyl tablecloth
- any flour (just make sure players won't be allergic to it)
- a dinner knife (long but blunt); a pallet knife or cake slice is also good

TO SET UP . . .

1. Lay the tray or tablecloth out on the floor.

2. Put the flour into the pudding bowl, packing it in tightly.

3. Tip the flour out into the middle of the tray or tablecloth – like a sandcastle.

4. Stick the matchstick in the centre of the top.

5. Place the knife nearby and tell everyone to sit in a circle round the flour.

TO PLAY . . .

1. Each player takes it in turn to cut into the flour mound and slice off a piece of the flour using the knife. The 'slice' of flour can be any size!

2. They push the flour they've cut away from the centre.

3. Then they hand the knife to the person on their left for their attempt.

4. Keep going round the circle, cutting and removing flour until you've got a small column with the matchstick perched on top.

5. The person to make the matchstick fall into the flour has to then retrieve it using only their teeth.

There was a family dispute about how best to build the flour mound, so if the pudding bowl method isn't working out for you, try my dad's version, which is to use a palette knife to gently push and pat the flour into a rectangle-shaped 'cake' instead!

This recipe is not edible, but it is taste safe, so it's OK if little ones accidentally put it in their mouths.

SALT DOUGH TIC-TAC-TOE

Now the making of this game isn't a five-minute activity, although each element on its own almost is. I'm aware it's a bit faffy, though, and you might not be up for it. I like to create this over several days, so I find it's a good activity for over the school holidays, as we can do one element each day and stretch it out. Once you've created the game, you can spend five minutes playing it, and it'll last you for as long as you like – or, if you're like me, until you forget to bring it in from outside during a storm and the rain destroys the whole thing! We have lots of fun while it lasts so it's something I now do with the kids every summer.

MAKE THE SALT DOUGH:

First you need to make the salt dough. Here is a recipe the lovely Emma **@messylittlebugs** put on a guest blog on my website:

GRAB:

- ¾ cup of salt
- 1 cup of plain flour
- about ½ cup of water (just enough for the dough to come together)
- paint/pens to decorate (optional)

TO SET UP . . .

1. Mix the salt and the flour in a bowl and pour in the water, mixing until a ball of dough starts to come together. If you don't want to decorate later, you can colour the dough with food colouring by mixing it into your water before adding.

2. Then get your hands in and knead it together to form a smooth ball of dough. This takes about two minutes!

3. Shape it exactly as you would with play dough. Make ten small balls (to fit into an egg box) out of your dough.

4. Once your salt-dough balls are ready, pop them on a baking tray and into the oven at a low temperature (about 120°C).

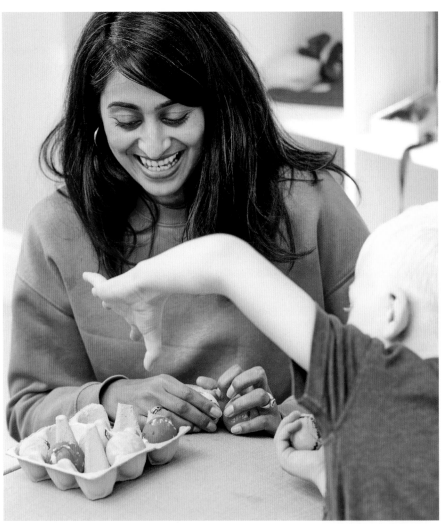

THE FIVE-MINUTE VERSION

If you don't want to bother with the salt-dough version, find some small pebbles and stones and paint them instead. Easy!

5. When your salt-dough balls have cooled, you can decorate them. You need to decorate five in one style and the other five in a different style.

6. You could easily just do two colours, or whatever you like. We did bumblebees and ladybirds. We painted one set red and one yellow and then I added the details on afterwards with a permanent marker.

7. Once you've painted them, you now need a large egg box. Not a standard egg box but a large one like you find at supermarkets. Often, if you ask, the staff at a supermarket will give you one for free. Or just cut up and tape two standard egg boxes together! You need a three-by-three hole grid, just like a tic-tac-toe grid on paper.

And there you have it. Now you can play!

TO PLAY . . .

1. One set of balls – bumblebees or ladybirds for us – for each player.

2. Just like tic-tac-toe, but instead of drawing in noughts and crosses, you pop the balls into the boxes, until one player manages to make a line of three the same.

I left this out and the kids and their friends picked it up constantly for a quick game. It was really fun to watch Florence, my youngest, constantly beat her elder brother at it because he was so busy concentrating on winning he forgot to block where she was going. It gave us many five-minute giggles and it could very easily be popped in a bag for **ON THE GO**. And this way, if it breaks or goes missing it doesn't matter. You can easily just make it again!

LACE RACE

This game is handy if you have a few older kids around who are a bit bored, and you want to keep their hands busy for a little while!

GRAB:

- a pair of shoes with laces for each player (their own shoes or borrowed)
- something that can be used as a timer, like a phone or watch

TO PLAY . . .

1. Each person needs a pair of shoes with laces.

2. Split everyone into two equal teams. If you have an odd number of people, someone can be the referee; otherwise, one of the players can also take the role of referee and be in charge of the timer while playing.

3. The teams gather their shoes and put them in a pile. Then swap piles, so each team has the other team's shoes.

4. The referee shouts, 'Ready, steady, go!' and starts a timer for two minutes.

5. Each team has to knot the laces of the shoes in front of them together as quickly as they can, tying them in as complicated a knot as they can manage in the time. They don't have to be in pairs either!

6. When the time is up, the referee shouts '**TIME**' and each team must run back to their own shoe pile and start untying the knots as fast as they can.

7. The first team who all have unknotted shoes on their feet wins.

OUTDOOR GAMES

In the summertime, when the weather is fine . . . Which is usually about nine days here in the UK, but never mind. Let's make the most of it and get outside to play – preferably in big groups. Most of these games will be familiar from your childhood but I've included them here because we must treasure them and repeat them so they are never lost. Unfortunately, the culture of 'playing out in the streets' isn't what it used to be any more (yes, I am aware I sound about ninety-six!). But a friend on Instagram recently did a poll to ask her followers if their kids 'played out' after school and the response was almost 80% saying that no, they didn't.

I spent my childhood playing out with friends any chance I got, so I feel sad that so many children, for whatever reason, aren't getting that same magical experience I had. Obviously it depends on where you live – it's not easy if you live in an area with lots of traffic or limited outdoor space. However, there is a movement trying to change this, and if you go to playingout.net you can find out how you might be able to turn your street (almost any street!) into a safe space for children to play in. We are incredibly lucky and live in a community that has been designed for children to play in, and our children go out to play a few times a week.

Games like these are a rite of passage for them all . . .

DUCK DUCK GOOSE

A school playground classic. We used to play this for hours, and it's about time I introduced it to my kids for when they're playing out with their neighbours!

1. Everyone sits in a circle except one person who is the tagger.

2. The tagger walks around the outside of those sat in the circle, lightly tapping each person on the head and saying, 'Duck, duck, duck,' until they decide one person is a goose and they shout '**GOOSE!**' when tapping them.

3. The person tapped has to get up as quickly as they can and run a complete lap of the circle (as does the tagger), trying to catch the tagger. The aim is to run a lap and sit down in the now-empty space in the circle.

4. If the tagger gets there first, the person who was tagged becomes the new tagger and starts tapping heads again, saying, 'Duck, duck, duck . . .' And so the game goes on!

5. If the goose gets there first, the tagger has to start again.

It's best if you can take your shoes off, if possible. There's nothing nicer than running barefoot on a hot summer's day!

LADDERS

I used to play this at Brownies, and it was always one of my real favourites. It's easier to play than it is to describe on paper, so feel free to pop to my website **fiveminutemum.com** for videos if that's easier to see what I am going on about!

1. You need at least seven people for this game. One person is nominated as the scorer, and everyone else gets into pairs that sit opposite each other with their legs outstretched and the soles of their feet touching.

2. You're trying to create a 'people ladder' as per the photo opposite, so each pair sits beside another and all the paired legs make a ladder of rungs. Each pair is then given a number, with number one nearest the scorer, going up consecutively from there depending on how many pairs there are.

3. All the people on one side make up one team, while the people on the other side of the ladder are the other team.

4. The scorer shouts a number – 'number two' for example – and the pair that are number two must stand up and run up the ladder (hopping over the legs), then around the outside of their respective sides and then back up the ladder again to their place. The first one to sit down in their place again wins a point for their team.

5. The scorer calls a different number each time and also keeps score of which team wins the point and adds them up. They can also say things like 'hop' or 'backwards' to make it more challenging if they like.

6. Do as many rounds as you like. The winning team is the one with the most points.

TEA CUPS

This is a game I used to play as part of a warm-up in netball training, but it was always good fun for a run around, and is perfect if you have a gaggle of very energetic children on your hands. You can use cups, cones or paper plates to play this, or even (as we have here) empty flower pots.

1. Lay cups or cones out in an area. Put half of them upside down and the other half the right way up.

2. Divide the children into two teams. There can be as little as two players on a team. One team are 'right way round' and the other team are 'upside down'.

3. Set a timer for one minute and say '**GO!**'

4. Each team must run around trying to turn as many cups as they can the way that matches their team name. You can turn over any cup at any time.

5. When the timer buzzes, all players have to freeze while you count how many cups are the right way, and how many are upside down. The winning team is the one that managed to turn the most cups their way!

PROPER HOPSCOTCH

I wrote about hopscotch in my first book but it was a simplified version for learning numbers. This is the full and 'proper' version purely for competitive fun and is dedicated to my beloved Nan, who used to play this for hours with me outside her little house.

1. Use some chalk or masking tape to mark out a hopscotch grid as per the photo. Each player has to find a small rock or stone.

2. From a set distance away, take turns to throw your stone to get it to land in the correct number box. You all start by trying to land your stone in the box marked number 1.

3. Once your stone lands in 1 you must jump **OVER** the 1 box and hopscotch your way to the end (by jumping and hopping along the numbered boxes), then turn round and hopscotch back to where your stone is.

4. You must pick your stone up without stepping outside of the hopscotch grid or into the box your stone is in, and again jump over the box the stone was in to return to the beginning.

5. Once completed, you have 'got' 1 and may now move on to trying to 'get' number 2.

6. You keep going, getting each number consecutively, until you have done all ten. You must retrieve your stone each time without stepping outside of the hopscotch grid. Sometimes this means you will be standing on one leg as you bend to collect it.

7. If you do wobble and step outside, that go is void and you must try to 'get' that number again.

GOLF-BALL BOULES

We have a set of garden boules which is a fab garden game for a group. However, it is very heavy and I found I would rarely take it out with us to play with for that reason. So I came up with this alternative idea for taking on walks and picnics, which meant we could play boules wherever we went.

Now it helps if, as we do, you have golfers in the family, or people who go for walks near golf courses. Grandad would often bring back random balls he had picked up and found. Eventually we had enough of a collection for a different colour each – with one ball to be the 'jack'. I kept these balls in the bottom of my rucksack over the summer, just in case we were at a park or beach and fancied a quick game. (It doesn't need to be golf balls, though! You could play this with any random balls you have at home, but it helps if they are all the same size and weight, and I found golf balls to be the best alternative.)

TO PLAY . . .

1. Select one ball to be the jack (or a rock or leaf will do) and throw or place it randomly in front of you. Agree a throwing spot or line.

2. All take one of the remaining balls and attempt to roll/throw it as close to the jack ball as you can.

3. If you have enough balls, have a second shot each.

4. The winner is the one whose ball was closest to the jack. They get a point (two, if you threw twice each and both their balls are the two closest) and get to throw the jack ball for the next round.

5. The overall winner is the first to ten points.

WATER GAMES FOR HOT DAYS

A water fight is a sure-fire way to turn up the volume on any hot sunny day. Shrieks will pierce the humid air once water starts being thrown about and there is nothing that my kids love more than squirting Mummy and Daddy with water, and seeing us run away shouting, 'Oi!' Here are a few ways to enjoy water fun outside as a group or family when you need a way to let off some steam.

FLIP CUP

You can play this game a variety of ways, but this one includes water. You can either play this in teams or as a one-on-one game.

GRAB:

- lightweight cups (paper ones are sometimes OK, but plastic works best)
- pen and paper
- a bowl
- masking tape (for two-player version)

TO SET UP . . .

1. Fill as many cups with water as there are players and create a line of the filled cups for each team. So, if there are eight people playing – four on each team – then fill up eight cups and make two lines of four. Put the filled cups on a table.

2. On a bit of paper write different body parts – one part for each player, so if you have eight players you write eight body parts – like foot, arm, head, shoulder and so on . You can repeat some if you like, or if you have lots of players.

3. Then cut the paper up so there's one body part listed on each piece. Fold the pieces up and pop them in a bowl, which you put on the table.

TO PLAY . . .

1. Get everyone to split into two teams.

2. The first player runs to the table with the cups. They must pick a body part out of the bowl and read it aloud.

3. They then have to pick a cup and tip the water over that body part on themselves.

4. Next, they place the cup on the edge of the table so part of it is overhanging the edge, and quickly flip it with their hand so that it lands the correct way up on the table. They can attempt this as many times as they like until they have done it.

5. Once they've successfully flipped it, they must run back to their team and tag the next person to do the same.

6. The first team to have all cups successfully flipped wins and gets to refill their cups and throw water over the others!

TWO-PLAYER SET-UP AND PLAY . . .

1. Get five cups per player. One player uses a pen to mark a cross on the bottom of their five cups. Grab one further cup and fill it with water.

2. Use masking tape to mark out a noughts-and-crosses/tic-tac-toe grid on a table.

3. Line all the cups, upside down, along the edge of the table, so the edges are overhanging slightly.

4. Say '**GO!**' and both players have to try to flip their cups over one at a time, by hitting the overhanging edge with their hand, to make them land the correct way up on the table. Keep repeating the attempt with the same cup until it's successful.

5. Once a player's landed a cup successfully the correct way up, they can use that cup to place it on the grid wherever they like, obviously with the ultimate aim to get three of their cups in a row.

6. Both players frantically keep flipping cups and placing them. When someone wins the game with three cups in a row, they get to grab the water-filled cup and throw it on the other player!

SPLAT

There is nothing more satisfying than throwing something and it making a lovely splatting noise. This is the simplest of ideas, and yet often it's the simple ones that are the best.

GRAB:

- a bucket
- some paper towels, sponges or cloths
- chalk

TO SET UP . . .

1. Using the chalk, draw a target either on a path or a patio.

2. Start with a 100-point small bullseye circle, then draw concentric circles going outwards as the scores get smaller.

TO PLAY . . .

1. Dip the paper towels/sponges/cloths into the water and take it in turns to splat it at the target.

2. Paper towels work best as they will often stick to the target where they land.

3. Take five shots each, then add up your scores.

4. You could then mix it up by:

- throwing backwards and through your legs;
- throwing blindfold;
- throwing with your least strong hand;
- playing a few rounds and each having a 'joker' to play, which you must declare before beginning that round, and which means your scores on that round are worth double;
- making one of the ring scores a minus number.

A great tip for water balloons and general water play is to get one of those large refillable water tanks, with the little tap. You can set this up in your garden so the kids can have easy access to running water to fill their balloons or use however they like.

There's a second game we play after this one. In order to pick up all the little bits of popped balloon around the garden to put in the recycling, I give the kids a cup each with a line drawn on it in wipeable marker. I say that the person who can fill the cup with balloon bits up to the line wins an ice cream or lolly. It works every time!

WATER BALLOON HUNT

Water balloons are great fun on their own anyway. But if you've got some spare and fancy mixing it up a bit, here is a game I made up for the brand Bunch-O-Balloons to advertise their product, but we still play now.

GRAB:

- a bucket of filled water balloons (this is why I love Bunch-O-Balloons, because filling them takes less than five minutes)
- some paper, pen and scissors
- chalk
- a bowl

TO SET UP . . .

1. On the paper, write something for the kids to find. It depends on their ages and how you wish to do it, but it could be shapes, numbers, letters or words – whatever you like, but they all need to be different.

2. Now write the same things you've written on the paper in chalk all around the garden. On walls, shed doors, on the ground – wherever you can, but not on a greenhouse or anything breakable.

3. Cut up whatever you've written into individual tickets, fold them up and pop them in the bowl.

TO PLAY . . .

1. The kids have to pick a ticket at random out of the bowl.

2. Grab a water balloon out of the bucket and find the matching thing to splat with the balloon. They have to make the chalk disappear.

3. You can either just play for fun or make it competitive with each child having the same number of tickets and saying, 'Ready, steady, go!'

VIDEO-CHAT GAMES

For many of us, 2020 and 2021 were the years when celebrations and get-togethers couldn't happen in person due to the global pandemic, so calling our loved ones to chat over an online video call was the closest we got to them. It was incredibly difficult at times, not being able to reach out and cuddle those we most wanted to be with. But what was also really hard, I found, was having video calls with kids around. They either shouted over everyone non-stop, faces up close to the screen, or took one look at the computer and then wandered off, because talking to Grandad on a tablet just wasn't the same.

So I started to think up ways we could connect and chat with loved ones over video calls in a way that children would also enjoy and engage with. I also noticed that kids found it difficult to speak to each other online, but once a game was involved everyone wanted to be a part of it and it became much easier. So here is what I came up with to make sure our video chats went beyond the usual 'nothing to report' chit-chat and into the realms of laughter and joy.

1. FINDING GAMES

You can do this lots of ways. One parent has a list of simple things, for example a spoon, teddy, block, pyjamas, toothbrush, leaf. They shout out the item and one child from each family has to go and find it as fast as they can. First one back to the screen with it wins a point for their family. Or, if you're playing with older children, you could hold up a letter and the kids have to find something beginning with that letter. Or you could do it as a relay and one child from one family finds it, then tags in a child from the opposite family to go and find it too. This is good if you have lots of young people on the video call.

2. BOARD GAMES

If both families have a set, board games like Twister can be fun to play across the airwaves. Both pull out your mat and spinner, spin for each other and shout what the other family has to do. First to collapse into a heap of giggles has to do a forfeit, like twenty star jumps. If you have the same sets of other games like Guess Who? or Battleships (see my version, Grids and Battleships, on page 215) you could play these too. You could even make your own matching board games out of scrap cardboard and move each other's pieces along as you play.

3. TOY TOMBOLA

This is one of my own games. One family has the 'tickets' (bits of cut-up paper with numbers on) and the other family has the line of toy 'prizes'. Select a ticket and tell the other family what number it is, and they count along their line, then show which prize has been won. Then swap over so the first family now has a line of toys as 'prizes' and the other family select the tickets and see what they've won. For older ones, make the tickets sums with the answers between one and twenty. You could even have a few booby prizes like a head of broccoli or a cup of mud and see if anyone 'wins' those, and perhaps a golden prize where if the number for that one is drawn out the child instantly 'wins' them all.

4. BINGO

Put numbers 1–50 into a bag. Then each write ten numbers you would like on a bit of card. One family pulls the numbers out and everyone crosses it off if they have it on their card. First person with all theirs crossed off shouts '**BINGO!**' Play again but this time the other family can draw out the numbers if you like.

5. PUPPET SHOW

Set the camera up so that the kids can sit under it and not be seen. Give them some dolls and teddies and set a five-minute timer. They act out a funny puppet show for the other family. Then swap over once the timer goes off. Make sure you give rounds of applause and take bows with all the 'actors'!

6. GUESS THAT TOY

One family goes and gets a toy and hides it off-screen. The other family gets to ask ten questions to try to guess what toy it is. You could also do this with well-known books. Once they get it or give up, do a big reveal!

7. DANCE-OFF

It can be fun to have a disco with another family! For more structure, you can play musical statues or musical bumps. One adult takes control of the music for one game – for both families! – then you swap over. I don't tend to make people sit 'out' when they come last in these games. Instead, I give the first one to sit down or freeze a point and the first to get to five or ten points wins the game so everyone can continue playing and dancing throughout. I am also sneaky and make it super close and exciting with my point decisions.

8. THE GENERATION GAME

Do you remember this TV show? Each family gathers up twenty random items (one must be **A CUDDLY TOY!**). At a steady pace, like a conveyor belt moving, pan the camera along the items to show them all to the other family one at a time, saying what they are as you go. Or, if you prefer, pick them up one at a time and hold them up to the camera. Then set a timer for one minute. The other family has to try to remember as many items as they can in that minute. Each time they shout out a correct item, say yes and chuck that item into a pile. At the end of the minute, see if they got them all. A great game for all ages.

9. READ ALOUD

Find a book you all have and read a page each. Perhaps while one family reads aloud, the others could act it out. Or join in with the sound effects if it's a story like *We're Going on a Bear Hunt*. Or even make up a funny story about your families and call each other to share the story of your own imaginary adventures.

10. BUDDING ARTISTS

Draw a portrait of each other and then reveal them. Perhaps set a timer to make it more of a challenge. Or call out an object and see who can draw it quickest – and best!

11. WORD GAMES

Play Would You Rather . . .? or other word games. (For ideas of what to ask, see pages 204–205.)

12. DO YOU KNOW?

How much do you know about the other family? Ask a question about one of them – favourite colour? Favourite smell? Favourite meal? Then both sides write an answer on a bit of paper and then hold them up. Do they match?

ON THE GO TO FORMAL OCCASIONS

FORMAL OCCASIONS

WEDDINGS

FUNERALS

FORMAL OCCASIONS

Sometimes family celebrations involve ceremonies. Be they for religious or cultural purposes, quite often something ceremonial requires everyone to be somewhat quiet and relatively serious for a little while. I'm thinking in particular of weddings, funerals and christenings, but obviously the list for many of you could be much bigger if, for instance, your place of worship is a big part of your life – and I know not all ceremonies require quiet. Different religions often have very different sorts of ceremonies too.

However, something that doesn't often mix that well is children and sitting still and quietly. A friend of mine's daughter once marched herself down the aisle on a Sunday morning to inform the vicar mid-service that she needed a wee-wee. It was something we all very much enjoyed hearing about over coffee the following week, because quite frankly we have all been there – not necessarily in a church, no, but trying desperately to keep a little one entertained during a quiet or formal moment.

So, over the next couple of pages I have included some anecdotes and tips around what I have done for times like this, on the few formal occasions we have attended with children in tow. We often try to leave them at home with willing babysitters, but this doesn't always make for an easier life, as I once had to pump breast milk while standing in the catering tent, as the staff washed up next to me. It was the only power socket for miles around!

WEDDINGS

My husband and I got married when our children were two and four years old. Our choice was to employ two of the staff from their nursery to be nannies for the entire day, looking after them so that we could relax. I know this is also a service you can specifically find online if you wish to – there are childcare professionals who specialize in wedding day-care.

My go-to for ceremonies has always been **LOLLIPOPS**. At our own wedding, there was a little bag of treats under Ewan and Flo's seats, waiting for them at the end of the aisle. They both sat on grandparents' laps licking lollies while we said our vows. (I avoided any brightly coloured ones as no one needs sticky red strawberry hands and lips combined with smart outfits!)

Before that, when we went to other weddings when they were smaller and couldn't quite manage lollies, I took raisins or a little tub of cereal to keep them occupied. As a guest with a little one I always sat as near to an exit point as I could, ready to make my escape should it all go wrong. At some point, all parents have experienced the pain of being the guest with the crying baby that they're desperately trying to soothe. It feels like the harder you try, the louder they scream, as your heart beats out of your chest with fear or embarrassment. But don't forget: every other parent who can hear them will most likely just be relieved it isn't their own child for once and you will have their full sympathy and understanding.

Another thing I've done is ask babysitters or grandparents to look after the children at home during ceremonies where I think the kids won't be able to cope with being still or quiet. Then I've picked them up for the noisier part later when they're free to be a bit more boisterous.

Lastly, and this will sound very obvious, I've found it's massively helpful to explain to kids how the ceremony will go and to talk them through why we must be quiet. It's also useful to show them a few child-appropriate videos online if you can. Obviously for a toddler this might be futile, but you can also prepare them through role play. Get out some of their toys and set up a wedding. Show them how when they're saying, 'I take you to be my husband/ wife,' all the other guests are *shhhh!* Then, once they've said, 'I do,' make everyone cheer and show them how you all have a party and eat cake. (Most kids are willing to do whatever you ask for a bit of cake!) There are some lovely books about weddings too. I bought our kids *The Scarecrows' Wedding* by Julia Donaldson, but there are plenty more.

THINGS IN MY CLUTCH BAG ON A WEDDING DAY

- a lollipop or small snack for each child

- a travel-size pack of wipes

- a pack of tissues

- a small fidget toy for each child (see how to make your own from balloons on page 25 or just use a blob of Blu-Tack)

FUNERALS

I have never taken my children into a funeral ceremony itself, but I know that sadly many of you have had to. If I were to go to one with Ewan and Florence, I would follow the same process as if we were going to a ceremony like a wedding. Explain clearly what will happen and why people might be sad and crying, and load yourself up with the same distractions as for a wedding to keep them as quiet as possible.

Bubbles are crucial for times like this. At my husband's gran's funeral, he attended the ceremony with his family while I took the children to meet him at the wake afterwards, and while everyone was gathering themselves and getting cups of tea, I took the children outside for a bit. I blew bubbles that they chased for a good fifteen minutes. I could see everyone inside smiling as they watched them through the window. Never underestimate the power of a tiny pot of bubble mix in your handbag! And if you have Blu-Tack (or any other sticky tack), you can use that to hold the bubble bottle steady on a table or floor so the kids can dip in and out without knocking it over.

IN A BAG FOR AFTER ANY FORMAL CEREMONY

- a **TAT BAG** each (page 14)
- tiny pots of bubble mix – I save the ones from party bags
- a change of clothes each

4

ON THE GO IN TRICKY TIMES

TRICKY TIMES

MOVING HOUSE

MOVING DAY

NEW SCHOOL

POORLY PARENTS

HOSPITAL STAYS

TRICKY TIMES

There are times in all our lives when things get tricky. There is no straightforward path ahead of us; the road looks tangled and messy. For some, this could be for a long period of time and for others the tricky times ebb and flow like the ocean tide. Now, I don't have any qualifications that make me a seasoned expert on managing tricky times – I just try to learn as I go along. I think, for me, what makes a tricky moment so difficult and exhausting is that it immediately throws me back into the 'I don't know what I'm doing' part of parenting.

I am not a psychologist, nor someone who claims to know everything there is to know about mental health. I am a mum. And through everything that I have experienced, no matter what the circumstances, I've found a way to play. It doesn't matter if my anxiety is at its highest peak or if I am so glum that I feel the creative sparks in my grey matter have upped and left. I have and always will find a way to play. Because **PLAY** is what brings us back to ourselves, and connects us to each other, and I have often found that in the trickiest of times that is what we need most of all.

MOVING HOUSE

When my eldest, Ewan, was six and Florence was four, we decided to move from the north-west of England to the south-east to be nearer to my family. This obviously meant not only moving house, which is enough of a faff in itself, but also moving to a completely new town and moving the children to a new school.

We were heartbroken to leave our old town and school. We had really appreciated how lucky we were to be raising our two children in such a beautiful part of the country, and then when they started at the local school our gratitude only grew as we watched our children flourish under the kind, supportive supervision of wonderful teachers.

So, when it came to moving, we frequently asked ourselves:

WTF ARE WE DOING?

But we did know. We wanted to see our families eating together for Sunday lunch. We wanted our relationships with them to be the kind that meant they could pop in unannounced for a cuppa when they were just passing by. So we put an offer in on a house round the corner from my parents and began to make plans.

Whatever your reasons might be for moving, I found repeating them to myself helpful.

I can't claim to be any kind of expert on this. We've done it once and shan't be doing it again anytime soon, but there were a few things we did that I think ultimately helped the kids with such a big life change and I wanted to share them, as it's something I am frequently asked about on social media.

1. TALK EARLY ON

The first thing we did was prepare the children early. About six months before we eventually moved, we asked them how they would feel if we were to move house. We asked them how they would feel about having a new home, and talked through the pros and cons. We asked them if they would prefer to live closer to Nanna and Pops, and what that would mean to them.

We then also shared our own ideas and thoughts. We told them Mummy and Daddy had been thinking about perhaps moving, why *we* thought it might be good and why we also thought it might be difficult. We began this conversation very early to show we were including them in the thinking and decision-making process.

Obviously we made no promises to them. For Ewan and Flo, we kept the discussions initially hypothetical (talking about 'what if', rather than 'when'), and we often let them think on it for days or weeks at a time before bringing it up again. All the while, we had to crack on with arranging solicitors and house valuations, and all the necessary serious stuff that you need to start doing well before you're even close to confirming a house move.

2. MAKE A LIST

Once we knew we were very likely to be moving, we asked the children to write down or tell us the things they were excited about. In our case, the move meant a bedroom each – they had previously shared – and so that often came up in their lists, especially as we'd asked them if they wanted their own rooms, which they did. We then continued to ask them about decorating their new rooms to give them something positive to focus on. They also wanted a treehouse, but we had to remind them that not everything was possible!

3. DON'T IGNORE THE CONS

We also encouraged them to discuss the changes they thought they might find hard. The people they might miss. How they might feel about starting at a new school. We did this by telling them how we felt at first. The things we were sad about saying goodbye to and the people we knew we would miss. Once we started this, they began to join in the conversation too and we all shared and talked about it being OK to feel sad or worried about that. We would frequently have this conversation over dinner or on walks.

4. MAKE A MEMORY BOOK

I bought the kids a large scrapbook each and filled it with memories from their current school. I dug out certificates they had been given; I printed out photos of them with their classmates from the school website, and of sports days and nativities from my phone. Then, two weeks before their last day at school, I gave it to their teachers and asked them to write whatever they liked in it and to ask any children if they might like to do the same. They both came back **FULL** of beautiful things (that made me sob!), including messages from previous teachers and the head teacher, gorgeous photos I'd not seen before, little drawings and notes from their classmates. These scrapbooks are really treasured, and Florence even keeps hers by her bed to look at regularly.

MOVING DAY

When Ewan was around fourteen months old, we moved house for the first time as a family. Due to problems with the date of our move, we lost the deposit we had put down on a removal company, and at the last minute had to not only pack up all our stuff into boxes but then ask favours of friends and family to help us move everything too. Fortunately a friend had a large van, and my parents stepped in to help shift and lug boxes and furniture. And so – with a toddler in tow – we moved across town over two days.

NOT RECOMMENDED!

We of course survived to tell the tale, and the pizza and prosecco we had while sitting on boxes once we'd moved every last thing into the new gaff tasted all the sweeter for it. Fast forward, however, to 2020 and we were on the move again, only this time it was across the country and in a pandemic. *This* time we were not only careful about when to book a removal company (and pay the deposit), we also paid extra to have them pack up our stuff. This was amazing for two reasons. One, it meant we could live exactly as normal right up until the day of the move, which was brilliant with two small children; and two, it meant I didn't have to do anything except unpack the other side!

HIGHLY RECOMMENDED!

Now I completely understand that not everyone can afford a removal company, let alone the packing costs. We certainly couldn't in 2015. However, if you can, it's definitely worth it. The two chaps who did our packing were like **MACHINES!** But if you are doing it all yourself, then over the next couple of pages are my tips for what helped us . . . Oh, and don't forget the bottle of something nice for when you've done it because, boy, will you deserve it!

1 Search Facebook and other online selling sites for boxes and packaging materials. People who have recently moved are often giving them away for free as long as you collect them.

2 Pack a **FINAL AND FIRST** box. This needs to contain the things you need the most, and therefore want to have to hand until the final moments in the old place and then first in the new one. I kept this box with me in the car rather than load it into the van so I had it ready as soon as we'd put the new keys in the door.

You can see clearly from the list below of what was in my **FINAL AND FIRST** box that my priorities in life include having a cuppa and going to the loo in a dignified manner. A fine set of priorities, I'm sure you'll agree!

FINAL AND FIRST BOX LIST

- the kettle
- a few mugs
- teaspoons
- teabags
- coffee
- tea towels
- squash

- kitchen roll
- kids' plastic cups and plates
- kitchen cloths
- cleaning spray
- toilet rolls
- hand wash
- hand towels

3 Keep your little ones' bed stuff with you too. After I had set up the kettle and made a brew, my next immediate job was to prepare the kids' beds. I had put everything from their beds in the old house into a bin liner –including teddies, comforters, etc. – so it was simple to locate it all. I didn't wash the bedding before or immediately after we moved, so that when we arrived their 'new' beds smelled the same. Kids often experience the world in a multisensory way, so I made sure I did everything I could to provide comfort and familiarity.

4 If you can, ask the old owners to leave blinds, curtains and curtain rails up. Even if they aren't to your taste, this can make it so much easier early on. If they aren't able to leave them, then my old friend masking tape is handy here. Use flattened-out boxes, bin liners, newspaper or tinfoil to black out bedrooms if needed, and make it your mission to get something up over the windows as soon as possible.

5 Let your little ones have your phone to take their own photos of the house you're leaving. They can go around taking photos of anything they wish to remember. You can switch on Guided Access, which locks them on the photo app only so they can't accidentally order seventy-five candlesticks for your new house. Just go to Settings and look for Guided Access. Chances are you'll end up with 150 photos of light fittings and blurry corners of rooms, but if it helps them process the move then it's all helpful.

6 For very little ones, the high chair can be useful to keep them safely in one place while you're unloading boxes. Overleaf are some activities for them in a high chair to keep them happy and busy.

7 Finally, let your kids play. There isn't a lot that's more fun for a kid than an empty cardboard box, so moving day is a true highlight! Turn to pages 152–153 for packaging games.

HIGH-CHAIR GAMES
(FOR WHEN YOU'RE UNPACKING)

Now those of you who are familiar with an old blog post of mine called 'Why I don't do games for 0–12-month-olds' will know exactly why the activities below are not my own. When my two were very little, my creativity was blunted by sleep-resistant babies, and it wasn't until they reached toddler age that I suddenly sprang into action with fun ideas and activities. So, if you are in a fog with your babies, please **DON'T WORRY**! I was too and it does end. Fortunately there are people who are **BRILLIANT** at coming up with ideas for very little ones, and one such person is my very good friend Becky.

Becky has been sharing lovely simple and brilliant early-years activities on her Instagram and Facebook pages for years as **@beckys_treasure_baskets** and one of her highlights and areas of expertise is definitely high-chair activities. So the credit for the activities below lies with Becky and her very specialized form of genius. If you have a little one who is still in a high chair and requires entertainment to perhaps keep them in there while you do something, then here are some of Becky's fabulous set-ups.

1 Get some small toys, such as plastic animals or small-world people, and use masking or washi tape to tape them lightly to the high-chair tray. Your little ones can then unstick them all and perhaps might enjoy using the tape to stick them together or back to the high chair again. It goes without saying that the toys should not be so small that they fit in little mouths!

2 Pop some pom-poms in water and freeze them in an ice-cube tray. Tip them out on to the high-chair tray for your little one to touch and play with. You could also freeze small toys, fruit or other baby-safe items for them to discover.

3 Tape leftover cardboard tubes or boxes (an empty tube of Pringles is ideal) to the sides of the high chair. Then put items on the tray that they can drop into the tubes or boxes, such as dried pasta, pom-poms, plastic cutlery, anything you like really.

4 Push some ribbons through a colander. Knot each end of the ribbons so that little hands can pull a ribbon through a colander hole and it won't come out. You can then turn the colander over and they can pull the ribbons back through the other way.

5 Pop some blobs of play dough (taste-safe recipe on page 27) on to the tray and stick some straws in each blob so they stand upright. Now your little one can pop cylinders or hoop-shaped items on to the straws. Good things to play with are penne pasta, Hula Hoops (the snacks, that is!), Cheerios or cut-up toilet-roll tubes.

6 Make some taste-safe paint using yoghurt and a drop of food colouring. Tape some paper to the high-chair tray and blob some of the paint on to it randomly. Now give your little one some vehicles to roll across the paints and make fun patterns. They might also like animals to make stompy splashy footprints.

7 Tie lightweight toys to a long scarf and tie the scarf to the high-chair tray where your little one can reach. Then, if they push the toys off the tray, they will be able to grab them again using the scarf.

8 Get out a loaf tin or similar item and pop elastic bands around it (over the open end). Now you can either put items inside it for your little one to try to get out, or give them things to post in between the elastic bands.

9 Get a whisk and some pom-poms. Load up the whisk with the pom poms. Let your little one whack away on the high-chair tray to try to get all the pom-poms out.

10 Give them a plastic child-safe knife and some very soft fruit, like a banana or very ripe avocado. Let them have a go at 'chopping' it up and then obviously it's a snack too!

PACKAGING GAMES

1 Make your own TV (and remote) from a box. Pop a box of dressing-up outfits and accessories nearby and keep changing the channels so they have to change characters.

2 Cut an arm-sized hole in the side of a box, pop five random items inside, and then seal the box shut with tape. Can the kids guess what's in it by just feeling around? Perhaps get them to match items to letters if they are learning those. Then let them put in five items for you to guess.

3 Save the paper that's been used to wrap items like plates – it's perfect for drawing and painting. Use masking tape to secure it to the table when they're doing messy play, to save your surfaces and make cleaning-up speedy.

4 Bubble wrap is always fun! My kids particularly enjoyed rolling over it on their scooters or walking across it with bare feet. I taped bits to the floor as sensory stepping stones too, or to let tiny ones explore it without the risk of them putting it in their mouths.

5 Punch out the bottom of a box to make a tunnel. Do this multiple times and slot them together to make a super-long tunnel. Give them torches to explore it, or balls and cars to roll through it.

6 Flatten out a box and draw a hopscotch grid on it. (See how to play hopscotch on page 113.)

7 Flattened-out boxes also make brilliant ramps for cars and balls, or slides for dolls and teddies. Have races or tournaments with them. When we moved in, I managed to unpack my whole wardrobe while the kids slid a big bag of soft toys down a cardboard-box ramp, seeing whose was fastest.

8 Get a box for each child, chuck a load of felt-tip pens inside and let your kids clamber in and paint a design on it. Afterwards give them a picnic dinner or snack in it. The best thing about a box snack is that any crumbs are easily captured! Winner!

9 If you draw something on cardboard and then tape over it in clear tape, your children can then draw over it with felt-tip or dry-wipe pens. This is brilliant for colouring in, for example, so I drew around my hands and added nails with a black marker. I then taped over that and Florence spent ages giving the hands nail-art designs, which could be easily wiped off with a tissue or cloth. But let your imagination run wild based on what your child likes best.

10 For the queen of cardboard ideas, visit my friend Sydney Piercey's Instagram account @sydney.piercey. She has so many fantastic ways of making incredible things out of just cardboard and tape. Her page is the perfect companion to anyone moving house or with an abundance of cardboard and small children to entertain.

NEW SCHOOL

One of the tricky things about moving schools is that the process is incredibly quick, because here in the UK you can't apply for a (state) school place until you have exchanged contracts (which comes right near the end of a house sale). So, we had made all these plans to move across the country but didn't have a clue which one of the schools we'd investigated our children would actually be going to. Once we had exchanged – a week before we finally moved – we then had to apply to local schools, hoping there was space at our first choice. Once we'd got the new school placements (phew – there *was* space at our first choice), we then had only ten days to accept them, because the rule is that kids must start school immediately upon acceptance of the place. It's all a bit chaotic.

We were very fortunate that we moved over Christmas so the children had the school holidays to get their heads around what the new school was going to be like. If you get any kind of choice as to your moving date, I would aim for a school holiday if you can. I used this holiday time as much as I could.

4

HERE'S WHAT WE DID:

1 Asked our new neighbours if any of the kids in the street went to the school Ewan and Florence were going to be starting at. They did, and we arranged to meet them so we could ask all about it.

2 Walked to the school and back to see the entrance and to practise our new weekday journey.

3 Looked at the videos and pictures on the school's website together to familiarize all of us with the new school as much as possible.

4 Asked the teachers if they wouldn't mind doing a brief video call to introduce themselves. (We weren't able to go in due to Covid restrictions at the time, but this video call worked really well as an alternative to a face-to-face meeting.)

5 Contacted the school about second-hand uniform because I couldn't order new jumpers for a few weeks. Getting it second-hand meant I could pick it up quickly and show the kids what it would be like.

6 Signed up to the school newsletter and email updates immediately so that I had all the information I needed about upcoming events that my children might be involved in.

In my previous book *Give Me Five*, I talk about drawing little hearts on your hand and your child's hand if they are nervous about being separated from you when first starting school. They press the heart whenever they feel worried or nervous. You tell them you can feel it and send back a cuddle through your own heart. When both children started at their new school, we drew hearts on them too. Some people have suggested sewing a tiny heart on the inside of uniform sleeves too so it doesn't ever get rubbed off, which is a lovely idea.

POORLY PARENTS

Sometimes us grown-ups who have responsibility for these young humans do **NOT** feel up to the job. It's just a part of life that we might sometimes think, *Not today, thanks*. I usually am hugely grateful to be a parent, but sometimes we just want to lie on a sofa all day long without someone opening our eyes and asking, 'How many farts do you think I've done in my lifetime?'

We might be poorly for any number of reasons – sometimes with illnesses unfairly thrust upon us such as morning sickness, flu or food poisoning (some examples of what I have parented through!). Other times it can be sickness of the self-inflicted variety, such as 'Mummy enjoyed a margarita or six and danced until 2 a.m. on the table and now I regret my life choices'.

Whatever the reason, sometimes we just wanna **LIE DOWN**. But kids, as we know, are very much always **ON THE GO**! So, aside from limitless TV and iPad time (yes, that happens too) or making an SOS call to grandparents or other willing babysitters, my only other tactic is to try a few of my favourite activities that involve sitting or lying down for as long as I can possibly get away with.

1. THE SALON

Let them loose on you with make-up and hairbrushes. You might end up with the face of a clown who's had a kiss with a bouncy castle, and hair like a Disney princess exploded, but if they're anything like my Florence it'll keep them quiet long enough for you to watch an entire episode of *Pointless*. Pedicures and manicures are also good for this. Just pop your feet on some newspaper and get ready to say, 'I can't move – my toes are drying,' for as long as possible.

2. DOCTORS AND NURSES

Crack out the toy doctor's set if you have one. If not, a toilet roll, some masking tape, a real thermometer (optional, not glass), a magnifying glass and something for prodding patients – like a wooden spoon. Lay some cushions on the floor, tell your kiddos you're very poorly, and lie down for as long as you can possibly milk it. Keep adding to your ailments! The only downside is you'll likely have to play doctor too at some point, but you can always say that the toys are poorly too and hope your kids continue the game by moving on to them.

3. STEAL THE KEYS

Get a bunch of keys and put them in front of where you're sitting. Blindfold yourself and pop out some cushions as stepping stones on the floor. Tell the kids it is their mission to steal the keys by hopping along the stepping stones (the floor is lava!). If at any point they make a noise, and you point directly at them, they are out. Then either they can go back and have another try, or a sibling can have a go at trying to steal the keys. The aim of the game is to go **SUPER** slow and **SUPER** quiet (and then Mummy can have a few minutes lying down with a sleep mask on). *Shhh!*

4. SLEEPING LIONS

I am yet to get this to work with my kids, but others have told me it does, so I'm popping it here in case your children are the type who will lie on the floor for as **LONG** as they can without moving. First to budge an inch loses. Last one lying still is the winner. My two just immediately jump up and say, 'I lose,' and then continue to bug me.

5. MOVIE DAY

Sometimes I like to say it's a movie day. We make popcorn and load up with drinks and snacks, I move the sofa round so it's directly in front of the TV, then I pull the curtains, turn off the lights and thank the Disney gods for its amazing app that gives me all the kids' movies I could ever want at my fingertips. My friend Abbie likes to ask her kids to make tickets too and she plays cinema music as they enter the room. It's **EXTRA** and I **LOVE** it!

6. BUCKAROO

Tell your kids you are a sleeping monster and lie on the floor with your eyes shut. They have to bring their toys and carefully, silently, balance them on you one by one. If they 'wake' the monster, you will shout, 'Buckaroo!' and sit up making all the toys fall off, and that person loses. Obviously you just lie still for as long as you can until you're covered in toys! Keep switching up who is the winner. Wink, wink.

7. MUSICAL STATUES AND BUMPS

The reason this game is excellent is because I just sit on the sofa with the TV remote. I put on a music channel and my kids dance around. All I have to do is occasionally pause it. They then either sit on the floor or freeze once the music stops, and I say which one gets a point. First to ten points wins if they want to get competitive.

We often pop into charity shops to buy jigsaw puzzles for the kids. They sometimes have stickers on the front that tell you if there are any pieces missing, and for a couple of pounds my kids are entertained by this 'new' toy for a little while. We return the set to the charity shop afterwards, so our house isn't cluttered up with puzzles they only want to do once. I see it like a kind of puzzle rental service – and you get to support a charity!

8. COLOURING

Now wait, I know, but hear me out. If I sit and do some colouring-in **MYSELF** and leave a selection of colouring books and pencils out nearby, more often than not my kids will join me and colour too. It's a very low-effort activity. But I cannot at any point suggest colouring, otherwise they will tell me where to shove it and that colouring is **BORING**. I just have to start doing it myself, and for some reason this miraculously works. Once they're hooked in, I can usually slip off for a bit too.

9. PUZZLES

Same deal as with the colouring. If I lay a few out nicely and start doing one lying on the floor, they will come and lie with me and join in. Plus, sometimes they get bored and wander off so I get to just lie among my pillow of puzzle pieces!

10. EARLY BATH

Any time of day, run a bath for them. You get to sit beside them or on the toilet with the lid down while they play and splash in the water. Some things I often add to make daytime bath times more fun (ahem, longer) are a couple of drops of food colouring, shaving foam in a muffin tin and some paintbrushes, Gelli Baff (stuff that turns the bath gloopy – it comes with a powder to reverse it back to liquid, so don't worry), swimming goggles, bath bombs (I always keep some in my cupboard out of sight for boredom emergencies) and bath lights or glow sticks so you can turn off the lights, play some music and make it into a disco bath.

HOSPITAL STAYS

Obviously there are times when there are more serious illnesses to contend with. Depending on how you look at it, we've been unfortunate enough to have been in hospital a few times with our children. I don't actually see us as unfortunate at all, because when we have been in, it has been for something that the incredible doctors have been able to fix, and we've come home with simply a 'Well, that wasn't much fun' memory and a few small scars. However, for many families this isn't the case. For some families the hospital is somewhere they are more frequently than home for large periods, or there is no simple fix for whatever took them to the hospital in the first place. And each and every time I've made myself a cup of tea in the 'parents' room' on a hospital ward, it is those people I am thinking of.

For us there have been a few reasons why we've had to make the dash to the hospital: Florence's head being split open, glued back together, splitting back open and finally stitched; Ewan having a non-blanching (doesn't disappear under pressure from a glass tumbler, for example) rash as a baby; Florence having bronchiolitis and being put on oxygen; Florence having sickness and a temperature that turned out to be an unknown infection. All were scary and horrible times that involved hours waiting in A&E, followed by overnight stays and admissions to paediatric wards. My brain played out the worst-case scenarios on repeat and I wished with all my might to swap places with my little one. *Please let me do it instead.*

On all these occasions, we got to go home. We have our incredible NHS, which, despite being put under constant pressure, is still always there to turn to when things get terrifying. And I am very aware of just how terrifying they can get, as I am sure you all are too. I have friends whose children either have or had cancer. Some of them are going through treatment as I type. Because of social media, I follow the journeys and lives of children with disabilities or complex medical conditions. I have family members who have genetic conditions that affect their day-to-day lives. For some, being in hospital is sadly just a part of life.

So, I want to pull together a few ideas of things to support those who might be in hospital, whether it's for the first time or the fiftieth.

Now here's the tricky part. For me, when my children have been in hospital, all I've wanted to do was let them watch TV or play on tablets/my phone as much as they wanted, because quite often I was **UTTERLY** exhausted. If that's what you want and need to do, then **DO THAT**! Florence flicked through old videos of herself as a baby for about two hours once as I curled around her on a bed, dozing off every few minutes. Do whatever you need to do to keep you and your little ones calm.

But if you're in for a few hours and they have maybe perked up a bit (once, after some IV fluids, Florence suddenly wanted to play but was still attached to a drip), then how do we entertain them? Often hospitals have a play area or room, but in pandemic times these were closed and not all children are able to visit them. So, what can we do from a hospital bed with what is at our disposal?

WHAT TO CHUCK IN A BAG IF YOU'RE HEADING OUT TO THE HOSPITAL

If your little one hasn't been well, or there's been an accident and you decide it's time to go to A&E, here's my list of things to grab as you head out of the door:

1. YOUR PHONE CHARGER

2. ANY COMFORTER YOUR CHILD HAS

3. A DRINK AND A SNACK FOR YOU AND THEM

4. A COUPLE OF TREATS YOUR CHILD LIKES
(*Preferably not chocolate as hospitals always seem to be super warm, so watch out as a bag of Buttons might liquidize!*)

5. TAT BAG

These are the crucial items, but I have also sometimes grabbed a tablet and headphones, my child's pillow off their bed, spare knickers/pants and toothbrushes for us both, something to read for me, and obviously if you have a tiny one, the standard nappy bag stuff too (nappies, wipes and a change of clothes).

VOMIT BOWL GAMES

In hospital you are often given cardboard receptacles if you are at risk of vomiting. If you have a small child who isn't about to immediately puke, you will most likely put said receptacle on your head in an effort to make them smile! However, later, once the risk of vomit has passed, you might want to play a few games with the unused cardboard bowl.

1. TISSUE TOSS

Screw up five tissues each, put the bowl a distance away and take it in turns to shoot your five tissue balls into it. Keep moving the bowl around the room for different challenges. Perhaps keep a tally of scores by writing on the side of the bowl.

2. FRISBEE CAPTURE

This one is best if your child is in their own room rather than an open ward! Put an item at the end of the bed or a short distance away. I would often use a small toy from the **TAT BAG** or their comforter, which I'd brought from home. Turn the bowl upside down and attempt to throw it in order to 'capture' the item. The aim is to make it land perfectly over the toy by throwing it like a Frisbee. Take it in turns, and the first one to capture the toy wins – then maybe move the toy for another go. Florence and I once played a version of this where we tried to make it land in the small sink that was on the other side of the room.

3. POSTING POT

For little ones, turn the bowl upside down and use a pen to stab a few holes through the base. Next, screw up bits of tissue, rubbish or any small items you might have in your bag (even raisins!). Let your little one post them through the holes, lifting the bowl afterwards to reveal them all underneath. Perhaps count as you go if they're at that age where they enjoy counting.

4. WHO'S HIDING?

Put five random items out in front of your little one so they can see them. Ask them to close their eyes, then pop one item under the upturned bowl. Can they figure out which one is hiding when they open their eyes? Obviously use more items the more challenging you wish to make it, but make sure they get to have a turn hiding too.

5. WHAT'S IN THE BOWL?

Get a sweatshirt or a cushion and cover the top of the bowl. Now pop an item inside so your little one doesn't see it. Ask them to put their hand inside the bowl without looking and have a feel to see if they can guess what it is. It could be a coin, your phone, a small toy, a tissue – anything you like that's to hand. Let them have a feel and guess, then if they like they can put something in for you to have a turn.

ON THE GO WITH . . .

THE FIVE-MINUTE BOX OF TRICKS
CREATIVE PLAY BOX
ACTION BOX
LET'S LEARN BOX
SENSORY BOX FOR LITTLE ONES
CHALLENGE BOX FOR OLDER ONES

. . . JUST ME
. . . A PEN AND PAPER
. . . MY PHONE
. . . MY WALLET
. . . A DICE
. . . SERVIETTES AND SUGAR SACHETS IN A RESTAURANT

THE FIVE-MINUTE BOX OF TRICKS

Sometimes when you're going away on holiday – or even just going to visit someone who doesn't have children – you might feel the need to take a load of toys with you to entertain your kids. This is a pain in the backside for two reasons. Firstly, because you have to gather the toys – which often take up more space than anything else you have with you. Then secondly, if you're like me, when you get home that bag of random toys will just sit gathering dust, as putting them away takes more than five minutes and you just cannot be bothered!

To avoid this circle of loathing, I have devised the **FIVE-MINUTE BOX OF TRICKS**. I first came up with this idea when I was asked to travel to London to promote one of my books and demonstrate the games to a group of parents and children – and I thought, *YIKES! I am definitely NOT a children's entertainer.* (That is a unique skill all of its own!) On top of this, I was travelling from Manchester to London by train and Tube, and so didn't want to take a massive suitcase of things, yet I needed to show as many of my games as I could with the fewest possible items. So I created a **BOX OF TRICKS**!

Now, whenever we are going away somewhere – camping, to stay with family members, a weekend away in a hotel – I pack a **BOX OF TRICKS** to entertain the kids instead of several bags full of random toys. I grab a small cardboard box – any will do, but a small shoebox is usually ideal – and I pack it with a few items that allow us to play **MANY** five-minute games.

Over the next few pages, I've separated the boxes into themes to help you out, but you can mix and match the items in any way you like to create your own **BOX OF TRICKS**. Or, if you like, you could create a **MEGA BOX** of all the items, then pop this book inside and play them all. It's completely up to you. The beauty of it is that the more you and your children play with the random items in the box, the more ideas spring to mind.

EVERY BOX HAS IN IT:

- masking tape
- pens
- colouring pencils
- about 10 pieces of plain A4 paper
- Post-its (or bits of paper and Blu-Tack)

THEN CHOOSE FROM THE FOLLOWING OVER THE NEXT FEW PAGES . . .

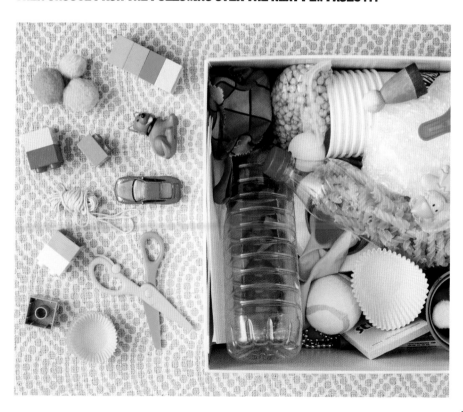

CREATIVE PLAY BOX

This is for children who like to sit at a table and be creative. It's ideal for little ones who love drawing, cutting, inventing and making things. You could just get everything out and let them go wild with all the items, or perhaps you might like to try a few of the activities I've suggested here.

INSIDE:

- essential items from page 169
- a scooping utensil (I save the ones that come with washing powder or milk formula)
- a plastic cup
- 2 different-sized spoons
- a small tub of dried chickpeas, or similar
- 1 egg box
- 6 paper straws
- a paintbrush
- a small tub of play dough (recipe on page 27)
- child-friendly scissors
- cupcake cases

PLAY:

1. CREATE PLAY-DOUGH COOKIES. Use a spoon to flatten the dough, then cut out shapes using the scissors or the scoop, and pop chickpeas on top of the 'cookies'. Pretend the box is the oven.

2. MAKE PLAY-DOUGH EGGS and pop them in the egg box. Write messages on small bits of paper and hide them inside the eggs, then 'crack' them open with a spoon and discover what's inside.

3. Use the pencils to make the compartments of the egg box different colours. **GO ON A HUNT** to find things that match the colour, then pop them in the compartments and create a treasure box.

4. Put some water in the plastic cup, then go and **'PAINT' OUTSIDE** with the paintbrush (or paint the box itself). As it dries, the 'paint' disappears!

5. **WRITE NUMBERS** on the egg-box compartments. Can the child count out the correct number of chickpeas into each compartment? If they are older, challenge them with some maths questions!

6. **MAKE ICE-CREAM CONES.** Cut up the egg box, so you end up with separate 'dimples' (apparently the official word for the cup-shaped sections that hold the eggs!) and the sticky-up cone-shaped bits that separate the 'dimples'. Colour in the outside of each 'dimple' and pop them on the upside-down cone bits to create 'ice creams'. (This idea came from cardboard queen Sydney Piercey.)

7. **HAVE FUN WITH CHICKPEAS!** Pierce holes in your egg box using the pencil, and pop chickpeas through them. Can your little one count how many you've posted? You could challenge older children to add them up too, or draw funny faces on the top and ask really little ones to 'feed' them.

8. Turn the play dough into eggs and have an **EGG-AND-SPOON RACE**.

9. **PLAY BLOW FOOTBALL.** Screw up some paper into a small ball, then blow it across a table using the straws. Shape the play dough to create goals – the first to blow the ball into their opponent's goal five times is the winner.

10. **PLAY TARGET PRACTICE.** Roll the play dough into a long sausage shape and cut it into five lengths before pressing each one into the floor in a semicircle shape. On five small pieces of paper, write out scores – for example 5, 10, 20, 50 and 100 – then place one on each play-dough semicircle. Take it in turns to flick the chickpeas at them along the floor, adding up your scores as you go on another bit of paper. The winner is whoever gets the most points!

11. On a smooth floor, make some shapes with masking tape – for example a small square, rectangle or octagon. Scatter the chickpeas around and give your child the paintbrush to **SWEEP** them into the shapes. You could even write numbers on the shapes, too, for the amount of chickpeas they need to sweep inside.

To clean up the lentils or chickpeas, just grab your blob of play dough and dab it on to them to gather them up. You can then pop the play dough into your food-waste bin later and make some more (page 27) when you need it again.

12. MAKE YOUR OWN FLAGS with straws, paper and masking tape. Use the play dough to make a stand for them.

13. DO PENCIL RUBBINGS. See what textures and patterns you can find wherever you are by putting a sheet of paper over it (secure it in place with the masking tape if you need to) and then gently rub the pencil over to see if the texture shows through.

14. MAKE BIRTHDAY CANDLES for a play-dough cake by cutting up a paper straw. Decorate with chickpea 'sprinkles/chocolate chips', too!

15. WRITE LETTERS OR NUMBERS on a bit of paper in bubble writing. Can your child colour them in, or perhaps fill them in using play-dough sausages?

16. MAKE PAPER DOLLS. Fold a piece of paper in a concertina, then draw the shape of a person with their hands going off the edge of the folds. Cut it out so the dolls all link, and then colour them all in however you like.

17. HOW MANY SCOOPS OF CHICKPEAS does it take to fill up the plastic cup? Can you see if it takes as many scoops of water?

ACTION BOX

This box is perfect for busy children who like to run, hop and jump, or who love to be competitive by trying to score goals and points! This is my favourite box because it is the kind of play I enjoy most. If you aren't sure which box your kid will like best, then my top tip would be to choose the one **YOU** enjoy most, because then you will be keener to get it out and play, which in turn will encourage your little ones to join in, too.

INSIDE:

- ■ essential items from page 169
- ■ 6 balloons
- ■ a ping-pong ball
- ■ 1 other small ball (like a tennis or squash ball)
- ■ 2 plastic or non-breakable plates
- ■ 2 toy cars
- ■ 2 small-world people (or other figures)
- ■ a plastic bottle
- ■ 10 plastic or paper cups

PLAY:

1. **CREATE A JUMPLINE** with masking tape on a floor where you have a bit of space. Challenge your little one to do a running or a standing jump from the line. Put another piece of masking tape down where they landed and write their name on it. Can someone else beat their jump, or can they beat their own best jump with a longer one? Use masking tape to record each jump to show their progress, or to allow a competition with friends and family.

2. **PLAY SKITTLES.** Stand the bottle at one end of the room and roll a ball to try to knock it over. If there are two or more players, take it in turns to sit or stand behind a masking-tape line and see how many attempts at

throwing or rolling it takes to knock over the bottle. The other player can return the ball as they count the attempts. Then swap over and see if the second player can knock it over in fewer attempts. If you're feeling adventurous, play it like a golf course by moving the bottle and masking-tape line for each 'hole'; keep tabs of the score, with the fewest shots per 'hole' winning overall.

3. DESIGN A RACETRACK out of masking tape for the toy cars to go along.

4. Twist a length of masking tape over and over so it becomes a bit sturdier and join the ends to make a hoop. Then set up a few of the small toys, the bottle, cars and anything else to hand as the prizes. Each player gets three throws each of the masking-tape hoop from a set distance away to try to land it over the items. **HOOP-LA!** You could even put scores on each item using the masking tape, or play it in teams.

5. STICK A SMALL-WORLD FIGURE ON EACH PLAYER'S BACK with masking tape. The game is that the players must try to pull each other's figures off their backs while protecting their own. The last person with their small-world figure still on their back is the winner – but once yours is pulled off, you are out

6. PLAY A NUMBER GAME WITH CARS. Make a small two-by-two grid out of masking tape. Write +2 on a bit of tape and stick it in the middle of one quadrant, then repeat with the three other quadrants but instead write −2, +3 and −3. Each player has a car, which they roll from a designated spot with the aim of getting it to stop in a quadrant. Start at zero (so minus scores are possible), and each time a player's car stops in a quadrant, either add or subtract the amount it lands on. Players take it in turns to roll their cars; the first to score exactly ten is the winner. Keep track with a bit of paper and pencil each.

7. Use the masking tape to make a **GIANT NOUGHTS-AND-CROSSES** grid. Use the cups as noughts and crosses: cups up the right way are noughts, and upside-down ones are the crosses.

8. PLAY A RELAY RACE GAME where players have to jump with a balloon in between their knees without dropping it.

9. Place the cups upside down and pop the cars and small-world figures on top. Use the balls to knock them off from a distance away, like a **COCONUT SHY**.

10. Blow up a balloon but don't tie it. Pull the neck of it apart and let a bit of air escape so it squeaks, then play **GUESS THAT TUNE**.

11. Alternatively, you can **PLAY BALLOON CATCH** – release the balloon and see if anyone can catch it before it hits the floor. If you have a few balloons in your box you could designate one to each child and the first one to bring theirs back to you wins a point. Or try to catch it in a cup!

12. PLAY SHOVE PLATE-PENNY. Mark five horizontal lines – just bigger than the width of a plate – across a flat surface. Players stand at one end and take it in turns to shove their plates along the surface trying to get it to land exactly within the lines without touching them. Once you have done this you have 'got' that section and can put a bit of tape with your name on the end of that line. First player to have a piece of tape in every tram line wins.

13. PLAY TABLE TENNIS WITH THE PING-PONG BALL, using the plates as bats. Create a 'net' with two upturned cups and the masking tape. If you've got little ones, use a balloon (which moves slower in the air so is easier to hit) and play tennis instead.

14. PLAY A BALLOON GAME. Create a large square target out of masking tape. Two people can play, each with a balloon placed on the floor. They have to hit their balloon with one of the balls to try to knock it into the masking-tape target. Each player takes turns to throw a ball at their balloon. The first balloon to land in the target area and stay there for three seconds wins. Alternatively, players can use their turn to knock another player's balloon away from the target!

15. Use the tennis ball, the masking tape and a wall to set up a game of **OLYMPIC WALL SQUASH** (see page 94). Again, littler ones can play with a balloon.

16. PLAY BALLOON KEEPY-UPPY. Blow up a balloon and try to keep it in the air for as long as possible. Mix it up by saying you can only use certain body parts such as elbows or heads. Count how many seconds each player can keep it up for.

17. Empty the box and blow up a balloon so it fits inside. Play a game where one player is trying to **GET THE BALLOON TO LAND IN THE BOX**, and another is trying to stop it. The players can only hit the balloon with one finger to attempt this.

18. PLAY PONG by bouncing the ping-pong ball into the cups. Set up a few cups at one end of a table or a hard floor, and the same number at the other. Players take it in turns to bounce the ball into the cups at the opposite end to the one they're standing at. Each time the ball goes in a cup, remove that cup from the game. The first player to bounce a ball into all their cups wins.

LET'S LEARN BOX

This box is full of games for learning, and I have tried to show some adaptations to the activities depending on your child's ability level. This box is ideal for little ones who are just being gently introduced to letters and numbers, and for those in preschool and first school years getting to grips with maths and English. Hopefully there are also a few games you can adapt for those a bit older to help with times tables and spellings, too. This is the perfect box if they are missing a bit of school while you're away and you want to do something to support your littles one's learning but not take away the fun!

INSIDE:

- essential items from page 169
- a marker pen
- 10 DUPLO® bricks or blocks
- a long piece of string or ribbon
- a piece of chalk
- 10 wooden clothes pegs
- a small beanbag (or a sock/bag with rice in it, tied with an elastic band!)
- a whiteboard marker

PLAY:

1. **PLAY NUMBER THIEF.** Write a number sequence on the Post-its and line them up in order. It could just be numbers 1 to 5, 10 or 20 for little ones, or the answers to a times table for older ones – whatever you like. Then ask your child to shut their eyes, take away one of the numbers and see if they can tell you which one is missing. Take turns to be the number thief.

2. **PLAY TOY TOMBOLA.** Lay out a peg, the chalk, the blocks stacked together, the Blu-Tack and the beanbag in a line. Make five 'tickets' using the pencils and paper. The numbers on the tickets need to be 1 to 5, or number

sentences for which the answer is between 1 and 5. So for example, one number sentence might be 2 x 2 = and another might be 6 – 3 =. Fold up the tickets and shout, 'Roll up, roll up!' Your child then chooses one, opens it to reveal the number or works out the sum, and then counts along the 'prize' line to see which item they have 'won'. Keep going until all prizes are won.

3. **PLAY WASHING LINE.** Tie the string between any two points (or use the masking tape if it's easier.) and then write letters on the Post-it notes or paper. Now use the pegs or tape to stick the letters on to the washing line. You could create anagrams to solve; get your child to correctly order the letters of their name or surname; ask them to try to create a message for you, or even make up a story using pictures to peg on to the line.

4. **MAKE A WRECKING BALL.** Tie the string or ribbon around the beanbag, and secure it somewhere high up, so the beanbag can swing freely about five inches (around ten centimetres) off the floor. Write letters or numbers on Post-its. Place a tower made of bricks near the wrecking ball with the Post-its scattered on the floor around it within reach. Take it in turns to swing the wrecking ball and knock over the tower, so it falls on to a Post-it. When it does, you can collect that Post-it and say the letter or number out loud. (If they want to, your little one can be the one to say it.) Keep playing until all the Post-its are collected, saying the letters or numbers as you get them, to help with recognition for your kiddo. The player with the most Post-its wins.

5. **USE THE BIT OF STRING OR RIBBON** to make the shape of a letter or number. Can they guess what it is and then have a go at one themselves?

6. **WRITE LETTERS OR NUMBERS ON THE PEGS OR BRICKS.** Hide them around the room. Now, on some Post-its, write the same letters or numbers for your kids to match. To make it more challenging, write a word on the Post-its with the hidden letter left blank for them to match, or a number sentence for which the hidden number is the answer. Can they find all the hidden items and match them to the Post-its?

7. **CHALK THE LETTERS OF YOUR CHILD'S NAME** (or other words they have to learn) randomly on the floor and see if they can hop or jump on them in the right order to spell it correctly.

8. **PLAY HOPSCOTCH**, either outdoors using the chalk or indoors using the masking tape. You can use the beanbag as your stone. See page 113 for how to play if you need a reminder.

9. **IF YOU HAVE A WINDOW OR A SMOOTH SURFACE**, write letters or numbers on it with the whiteboard marker and tell your child which they have to rub out. Or, if you have a little one who loves to do the opposite of what you say, jokingly say, 'Now don't you rub out the H. You must DEFINITELY not rub out a single H I am writing here – they are VERY important.' And then you turn away while they rub out the Hs, before you then do a mock furious routine ('Where are all my Hs!') while they laugh their mischievous little heads off.

10. **PLAY SILLY SOUP.** Write vowels on five Post-its, and consonants on the bricks. Pop them in the empty box and shake them, then ask your child, without looking, to pick one block, one Post-it and then another block. Line them up – what word have they got? Is it real or silly? If it's not real, what do they imagine it could be?

11. **CHALLENGE THEM** to see if they can find the five ways to separate a ten-brick tower by only using one break. They need to find 1 and 9, 2 and 8, 3 and 7, 4 and 6 and 5 and 5. Can they write down the number sentences? For example, 1 + 9 = 10.

12. USE THE PEGS TO MAKE PAINTBRUSHES by clipping to them things like leaves, grass, small bits of fabric or wrapping, flowers, soft plastic, newspaper – whatever you can to use for the brush bit. Can they use their 'paintbrushes' to write out letters or numbers with water on the ground?

13. WRITE LETTERS OR NUMBERS ON THE BRICKS with the whiteboard marker. Scatter them around the floor and use masking tape to mark out a throwing line. Take it in turns to throw the beanbag at a brick. If it lands on it, you write down the letter or number on your paper. First to write down all the letters or numbers wins.

14. PLAY A NUMBER GAME WITH BRICKS. In the empty box pop the ten bricks (separated), all the pegs and the beanbag. Tell your child each brick represents 1, each peg represents 10 and the beanbag is 100. Do a little jig and let some of the items hop out of the box. When they land on the floor, get your child to work out how much they've got. So if four bricks come out and seven pegs, the answer is 74. If the beanbag and one block come out, they would get 101. Let your child do the jig next and you count.

15. PLAY A LETTERS GAME WITH PEGS. Write lower-case letters on the pegs and upper-case on Post-its. Can your kids match the correct letters together by pegging them to the correct Post-it?

16. DRAW ROUGH PICTURES on the Post-its of things beginning with the letters on the pegs. So perhaps draw a cow, a bee, a flower, a hat, and a mop and see if they can peg the letters **c**, **b**, **f**, **h** and **m** on to the correct pictures by listening to the sounds.

SENSORY BOX FOR LITTLE ONES

I've written out some ideas for this box, but really with very small kiddos you can just use this as a kind of treasure chest for them to explore all the different things within! Exploratory toddlers only have a very short attention span, so my advice would be to either give them everything and let them look through the things one by one, or gradually give them individual items as they play to keep extending their exploring. Either way, I hope very much that this box buys you some peace, even if just for five minutes.

INSIDE:

- essential items from page 169
- a clear plastic bottle with dried pasta (like fusilli) inside
- a plastic cup
- 5 muffin or cupcake cases
- a piece of fabric (like a muslin or small scarf)
- 5 small-world (or other) figures or animals
- a long piece of ribbon
- a string of beads (from the Christmas box!)
- a handful of large pom-poms (about 10 is plenty)
- some bubble wrap (or any packaging)
- a wooden spoon

PLAY:

1. **PLAY WHICH ONE MADE THE SOUND?** Get the child to shut their eyes; then shake, tap or jiggle something from the box that makes a noise, and see if they can guess which item it was when they open their eyes. Let them do it for you so you can guess, too.

2. Use the bottle, the masking tape and the wooden spoon to make a **CATAPULT**. See if you can flick the pom-poms into the air. Where do they land?

3. Create a **SENSORY ACTIVITY FOR BABIES**. Tie the ribbon round something within reach and then tie a few of the toys and the scarf to it for them to play with. This is good for tying to a high chair, so toys don't get constantly thrown on the floor, or near a lying-down baby to keep them busy!

4. Likewise, use the masking tape to **TAPE A FEW ITEMS TO A TABLE** or on the floor nearby. See if they can peel off the tape and free the items.

5. Take everything out of your box, pop five items back inside and show your little one. Then ask them to shut their eyes while you take one item away. Can they **GUESS WHICH ONE IS MISSING?**

6. Pop the pom-poms into the scarf or fabric and tie it loosely so they are trapped inside. Get your little one to shake it or hold it while jumping around. **CAN THEY FREE ALL THE POM-POMS?** If it's big enough, you could tie it round their waist or leg, and they have to wiggle and jump to get them free.

7. Tip out some of the dried pasta into the cupcake cases and **MAKE PRETEND DINNERS**. Perhaps add some pom-poms or beads, too.

8. **WRAP UP** some of the items with the fabric or bubble wrap and ribbon – like a present – and let them open it to discover what's inside.

9. **PLAY SINK OR FLOAT?** Add some water to the cup and pop items into it to see if they sink or float. Have a guess together first to see what they think is going to happen.

10. PLAY POM-POM FOOTBALL. Tip the cup on its side and use the figures to kick the pom-poms into it to score a goal. Turn it into a competition if you like, with one kick each, taking it in turns and adding up your goals to see who's scored the most after ten kicks.

11. Tip the pasta out of the bottle and push the scarf or string of beads inside with one end poking out. Let your little one **PULL THEM OUT** again.

12. Poke holes in your box with a pencil and let your little one **PUSH THE PASTA** through the holes.

13. TELL A STORY. Get a few of your figures and then use the items in the box to make up a story. The ribbon could be a long road through a forest; the cup could be a boat; the string of beads could be the river; the wooden spoon could be a drawbridge to a castle! Send the figures on a little mission or adventure. You make one up first and see if your little one follows your lead to make up their own.

14. See if you can bounce or **THROW A POM-POM INTO A CUPCAKE CASE**. Have one each and try to challenge each other.

15. MAKE A RIBBON WAND by tying the ribbon to the wooden spoon. Twirl it around to make shapes in the air.

16. PLAY A MATCHING GAME. Draw round some of the items on a bit of paper. Can they guess which one goes with which shape and match them up like a puzzle?

CHALLENGE BOX FOR OLDER ONES

This box is for children who are aged five and up, and who don't want to play with play dough and 'babyish' things but still need to be entertained when the TV is switched off! This box is what I would take with me for Ewan (who is nearly eight), because it gives him plenty of opportunities to create and play but also is challenging enough for me to leave him with something to do while I am busy elsewhere.

INSIDE:

- essential items from page 169
- a small box of 15 coins – they can be real or pretend money
- a few LEGO®-style figures
- a dice
- Blu-Tack (or sticky tack)
- a handful of lolly sticks
- elastic bands

PLAY:

1. **MAKE PAPER AEROPLANES.** Add Blu-Tack or lolly sticks to them to see if it makes them fly further. You could even set up masking-tape targets for them to hit or land in.

2. **PLAY SNAKES-AND-LADDERS.** Draw your own snakes-and-ladders-style board game on the paper or the top of the box. Use the LEGO® figures as counters and the dice to play. You could include forfeits, too, such as 'jump ten times' or 'sing a song'.

3. Who can build the **HIGHEST TOWER** in five minutes using only the lolly sticks and the Blu-Tack? A LEGO® figure has to be able to balance on top.

4. **DO A PENALTY SHOOTOUT.** Make goal markings with the masking tape on a flat surface like a table or floor. Use Blu-Tack to attach one LEGO® figure to a lolly stick as the goalkeeper, then the other person uses their figure to flick a coin. Each player takes five penalties and whoever scores the most wins. A draw leads to a 'sudden death' shootout, with each taking one penalty after the other until someone wins.

5. **PLAY ODDS OR EVENS.** Lay out a strip of masking tape per player. On each strip, draw enough lines so that there are twenty boxes. Each player has a LEGO® figure as their counter. Roll the dice. If it is an even number, you move forward by the number you rolled. If it is an odd number, you move backwards by the number you rolled. The first to get to the end is the winner.

6. **MAKE A FORTUNE TELLER.** See pages 216–217 for how to make one. Once you have it, ask people to choose a number and move your hands that many times. Repeat three times and then on the fourth time, when they select a number, you open up that fortune and read out what it is. You can also do this with forfeits, too.

7. **PLAY NOUGHTS AND CROSSES** in as many ways as you like. On paper, with the masking tape in giant form, or with the lolly sticks as the board and coins and LEGO® figures as the counters.

8. Play the **COIN GAMES** on page 225.

9. Lay out a masking-tape target with a small bit in the middle as the **BULLSEYE** (with 50 written on it), then add consecutive boxes or circles around it with fewer points. Each player shoves or rolls three coins per go and sees what they score.

10. Give a LEGO® figure a **BLU-TACK MAKEOVER**. Create an outfit or a funky hairstyle for them, or accessorize. How about lolly-stick skis or stilts?

11. **PLAY NUMBER BINGO.** Grab a bit of paper each and write numbers 1 to 6 on them. Take it in turns to roll the dice. When a player gets a number, they can cross it off. The aim is to cross off all the numbers. However, if they roll a number they've already crossed off, their opponent can cross it off their list.

12. MAKE A LOLLY-STICK FIGURE out of what they have. Add Blu-Tack feet, use masking tape to fit the figure together, draw on them, give them elastic-band hair – get creative!

13. Play the **DICE GAMES** on pages 228–229.

14. HAVE A PARACHUTE COMPETITION. Create a parachute for a LEGO® figure out of paper and masking tape. The winner is whoever's parachute takes the longest to reach the floor when it's dropped by an adult (from the same height).

15. PLAY A BALANCING GAME. Tape together three lolly sticks so they make one long stick. Balance it over the top of the open box. Now each player takes turns to see how many items they can balance on the end overhanging the side before it flips off. Whoever balances the most is the winner.

16. MAKE A LOLLY-STICK CATAPULT with the lolly sticks and elastic bands (as shown in the photo). Flick LEGO® figures or Blu-Tack from it and see if you can get it to land on a target or back in the box.

ON THE GO WITH . . .

Life isn't all about the planned trips where we have the chance to organize absolutely everything. Sometimes I leave the house in a hurry. We might be out and about and I will realize suddenly that – although I have fortunately remembered my children – I have unfortunately forgotten the **TAT BAG** . . . **ARGH!** What to do? Well, we have to get creative with what's on offer. So here's a section dedicated to those times when I only have a . . . something, and need to find an inventive way to keep the kids busy. I'm thinking here of restaurants and cafes, grandparents' or friends' houses which don't have many toys, doctor's or dentist's waiting rooms, and all the other in-between times when we might have a few minutes to fill.

Now I know you might not necessarily have this book on you when this does happen, but hopefully if you give it a read-through then perhaps these ideas might nestle snuggly somewhere at the back of your brain (next to the 'pay the window cleaner' reminder) so when you're at a loss they'll come popping out. We can always live in hope – like my poor window cleaner who's still patiently awaiting payment!

Sometimes we also like to make up our own secret handshakes. I show the kids one and then they make up a handshake each and we practise them.

. . . JUST ME

What to play if it's just little old you and the kids? Well, we have two things at our disposal here. Our voices and our bodies! Now, there are a few games that we all might revert to in these moments. Here is a list of our faves . . .

1. ROCK, PAPER, SCISSORS AND THUMB WARS

2. I SPY
All versions including 'something that is [insert colour]', 'something beginning with [insert letter here]' and 'I hear with my little ear . . .'

3. I WENT TO THE SHOPS AND I BOUGHT . . .
Take it in turns to say what you bought and the next person has to remember what you bought and add something new. Keep going until it's a big long list!

4. SIMON SAYS
Someone gives instructions by saying, for example, 'Simon says . . . rub your tummy.' You must only respond with the action if it follows 'Simon Says'. If someone just says 'Rub your tummy' and you do it, then you are out.

5. MY FRIEND GEMMA'S COMPOUND GAME
Give out two clues for a compound word and see if they can guess it. For example, the word is 'butterfly' and the clues are 'something you spread on toast' and 'a buzzy annoying creature'. Can the kids guess what it is? Some other good compound words are: treehouse, buttercup, fireman, waistcoat, superman, football, cowboy, eardrum, sunflower.

The next few pages include some other ideas that may be useful for when you are **ON THE GO** and all you have is yourself to keep the kids occupied for a few minutes. Sometimes it feels like the pressure is **ON**, so having these in the back of my head has come in handy more times than I can even count!

WOULD YOU RATHER . . .?

I'm not sure this game really needs an introduction as I am sure you are familiar with it. Often when adults play, it involves a tricky choice between something rather disgusting and something revolting (a bit like a general election!). However, we can make it slightly more tame and use it as a conversation starter for kids. This is our go-to game for waiting around. Some of Florence's options made for funny car journeys recently – would we rather drink snot or eat ice cream? Not sure she's quite got the hang of it . . . so here are some ideas to get you going!

Have a pet dragon or a pet dinosaur?

Jump high like a frog or run as fast as a cheetah?

Live in a treehouse or a cave?

Be able to fly or be invisible?

Only eat ice cream for the rest of your life, or only have one ice cream a year?

Have a nose that can do magic or ears that can hear everything in the world?

Be super fast or breathe underwater?

Be kissed by a dolphin or have hugs from a bear?

Be able to go backwards in time or forward in time?

Build your own space rocket or invent the fastest car in the world?

Have pink bouncy bogies or farts that make a purple cloud?

Slide down a rainbow or float on a cloud?

Have springy feet that make you jump high into the air or elastic arms that mean you can reach faraway things?

Swim like a mermaid or fly like a butterfly?

Be on your own TV show or be a famous sports star?

Only see everything as one colour or all food tastes the same?

Be able to talk to animals or see into the future?

Have hair that grows super fast or hair that grows rainbow coloured?

TWO TRUTHS, ONE LIE

This is a good game to play with friends to reveal some saucy secrets. However, we can also play it with kids. 'HOW?' I hear you ask. 'They can't tell porky pies for toffee.' I know. But there is a way. And why not get a little educational? We can always sneak it in somewhere. I've written out some examples below that might be useful . . . Fun facts at the ready!

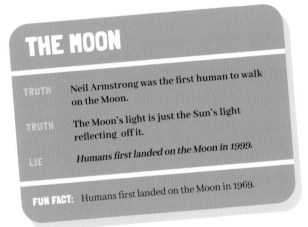

THE MOON

TRUTH   Neil Armstrong was the first human to walk on the Moon.

TRUTH   The Moon's light is just the Sun's light reflecting off it.

LIE   Humans first landed on the Moon in 1999.

FUN FACT: Humans first landed on the Moon in 1969.

DINOSAURS

TRUTH   Dinosaurs and humans were not alive at the same time.

LIE   The asteroid that killed the dinosaurs was six million years ago.

TRUTH   The word dinosaur means 'terrible lizard'.

FUN FACT: The asteroid hit Earth SIXTY-SIX million years ago.

WEATHER

TRUTH	Clouds are made up of tiny droplets of water or ice crystals.
TRUTH	The average-sized cumulus cloud weighs the same as a hundred elephants.
LIE	A scientist who studies the weather is called a rainologist.

FUN FACT: Meteorologists study the weather.

THE OCEAN

TRUTH	A blue whale can grow up to thirty metres long.
LIE	Great white sharks sleep on flat rocks.
TRUTH	Underwater exploration vehicles are called submersibles.

FUN FACT: The great white shark never stops swimming, to keep oxygen-rich water going through its gills. If it stopped swimming, it would drown!

ANCIENT EGYPT

LIE	Only kings (men) ruled in ancient Egypt.
TRUTH	The largest pyramid ever built was for King Khufu.
TRUTH	When kings (pharaohs) died, they were mummified.

FUN FACT: Queen Hatshepsut reigned over Egypt for fifteen years and was buried in the Valley of the Kings.

ELECTRICITY

TRUTH Lightning is a form of static electricity created inside clouds.

TRUTH Materials that allow electricity to flow through them are called conductors.

LIE *Electric eels aren't really electric.*

FUN FACT: Electric eels are electric in a way. They have lots of cells that store power like batteries and can shock their prey with stronger power than what we have in our plug sockets at home!

THE WORLD

TRUTH There are seven continents.

LIE The world's oldest inhabited continent is Europe.

TRUTH The island of Hawaii is part of the USA.

FUN FACT: Africa is the oldest inhabited continent.

WATER

LIE *Toilet water flushes to the centre of the Earth.*

TRUTH Roughly 70% of Earth is covered in water.

TRUTH The tallest waterfall is called Angel Falls, and it's in Venezuela.

FUN FACT: Toilet water usually goes down the pipes to a sewage plant to get cleaned and pumped back into rivers.

VOLCANOES

TRUTH Liquid rock inside a volcano is called magma.

TRUTH Volcanoes are more likely to happen close to where two tectonic plates meet.

LIE *You can only get volcanoes on land.*

FUN FACT: Volcanoes can occur under the sea too. (You might catch them out with the magma one, but liquid rock is only called lava once it reaches the surface! HA!)

SPORT

TRUTH On average, footballers run eleven kilometres in a game.

LIE *Ancient Greeks wore different-coloured shorts when they were wrestling. One red and one blue.*

TRUTH Nadia Comăneci scored a perfect 10 in gymnastics at the Olympics at age fourteen.

FUN FACT: Ancient Greeks wrestled in the nude!

There's a video on my Instagram page if you want to see this being played.

THE REVOLVING DOOR

This is a 'game' I invented with my kids one rainy day in our living room, and they ask for it again and again because they love nothing more than being chased and caught. However, I often can't be bothered to run around the house chasing them over and over so I came up with this in order to stay in one place but they still got the thrill of the chase.

1 Sit or kneel down in a space where you have plenty of room around you.

2 Lift your arms up and hold them out to your sides, parallel with your shoulders.

3 Now tilt your body in a rhythmic motion from side to side so each hand touches the floor once every three to five seconds.

4 The idea is that the kids have to run past you without being touched by your arms. If they get touched you can 'catch' them, which means I wrap both arms around them and say, 'Got you!'

5 They run loops around you, ducking under your arms as they go up and down, trying not to get touched.

6 I often speed up the arms or make the movements more random as the game goes on and they pause, trying to time their runs past me to miss the catching arms. I often also switch it up so that instead of my arms going up and down from the floor, I put one arm in front of me and one remains to the side (still both raised parallel with my shoulders), then I twist my body side to side so one side is 'open' with no obstructing arm, while the other side is 'shut' with my arm across it. Then I switch sides.

7 Sometimes I have also created a 'gate' with my legs across a sofa for them to try to run through before it 'shuts'.

I use all these movements as exercise for me, as usually after five minutes of playing this I feel like I've ticked 'do some Pilates' off my list for the week! Ha!

. . . A PEN AND PAPER

There are so many pen and paper games you can play. Lots of these I'm sure you'll know, but it's nice to be reminded sometimes for when we're **ON THE GO** and our brain space doesn't have the capacity for thinking up entertainment too!

1. NOUGHTS AND CROSSES

Obviously! But how about you play it as a tournament? Each player makes a list of four of their favourite characters from books or TV shows. Now each person picks one to be their player and their opponent picks one of theirs. Now play a game of noughts and crosses on behalf of that character. Write down the winning character at the end and pick a second character for the next game, continuing by playing with each of your four. For the next round, four characters will have won games. Pick two each. Again, play a round of noughts and crosses for each (if it's a stalemate keep playing until someone wins) and you'll have two players left for a grand final! Who will be the champion?

2. DOTS AND SQUARES

This is a classic that I used to play loads as a child – I think my mum taught it to me and we used to play it a lot on holidays. You draw a ten-by-ten grid made of dots. You each take turns to connect one dot to another with a single line. If your line forms a square, you put your initial in it. You keep taking it in turns to draw a line, forming squares until the whole grid is just squares with initials on. Count them up. The one with the most squares wins.

3. RASPBERRY FACE

This is our non-traumatic, child-friendly version of the game you might know as Hangman. Think of a word your kid can read/spell. Draw out as many dashes as match the letters in the word. Your child guesses a letter that might be in the word. If it is, you write it on the correct dash; if it isn't you write it underneath and draw a circle. Keep going until either the word is guessed or the child gets a 'raspberry' blown at them because each circle you have drawn will make a whole raspberry drawing as one circle makes a head, a second an eye, a third another eye, a fourth a nose and the fifth a mouth. When you draw the sixth, it's a tongue sticking out. Blow your raspberry!

4. LOTTO

This is easy to do. Rip up twenty small bits of the paper, write the numbers 1–20 on them and fold them up. Each player then takes another bit of paper and writes five numbers on it between 1 and 20. Take it in turns to select a number from the folded-up pieces. If you have that number, cross it off and keep selecting until someone has all five of their numbers crossed off and wins.

5. GRIDS AND BATTLESHIPS

Draw a quick grid and colour in certain squares on it. Draw another grid next to it and hand the pen to your child to see if they can copy it exactly the same. If they're older, play battleships. Draw a ten-by-ten grid each with numbers down the side and letters across the top. Each draw a one-square, three-square and five-square ship wherever you want on your grid. Use a menu or bag between you so you can't see each other's grid. Then take it in turns to call out strike co-ordinates (for example, 5D or 7F). Draw a cross wherever they shout and tell them if it's a hit or a miss. First person to sink all their opponent's ships with strikes wins. (Every square of each ship has to be hit.)

6. MAKE A FORTUNE TELLER

Can you remember making these as a child? Turn the page for how to make one.

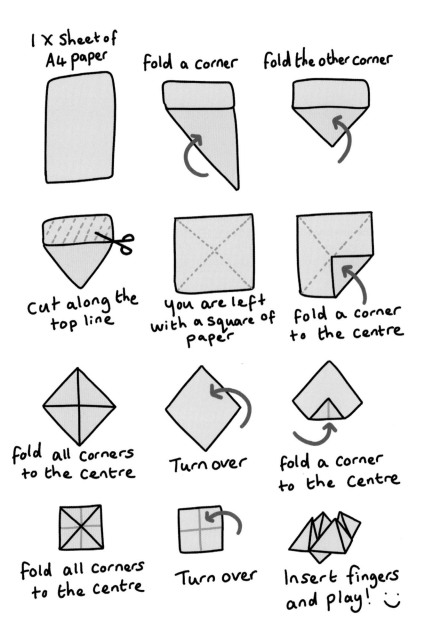

1 X sheet of A4 paper

fold a corner

fold the other corner

Cut along the top line

you are left with a square of paper

fold a corner to the centre

fold all corners to the centre

Turn over

fold a corner to the centre

fold all corners to the centre

Turn over

Insert fingers and play! ☺

MAKE A FORTUNE TELLER

GRAB:

- an A4 piece of paper
- a pen or pencil

TO MAKE . . .

1. Fold the bottom edge of your A4 paper to the right edge, then fold the right edge as in the picture opposite. Cut along the top of the paper where the folded-up edges stop. You will be left with a square piece of paper.

2. Fold the square in half diagonally, so the bottom-right corner goes to the top-left corner. Press the fold firmly (so you can tell where the crease is), then unfold so the paper is flat again. Fold it in half again, so the bottom-left corner touches the top-right corner. Like you did before, press the fold firmly and then flatten out the paper.

3. Fold the corners into the centre, where all the creases join. Press the folds firmly.

4. Keeping the corners folded in, turn the paper over and fold each corner into the centre as you did before.

5. You should have eight triangular flaps on the side that's facing up. Number them from 1 to 8. Then under each numbered flap, write a fortune, forfeit, joke or something to learn (like letters or words).

6. Turn the folded square over, and draw a different coloured dot on each of the four square flaps. Alternatively, write a number or a word if you don't have different coloured pens or pencils.

5

TO PLAY . . .

1. Fold the square in half firmly, so you have two squares on one side. Then unfold and fold the other way (again so you have two squares on one side).

2. With the fortune teller folded in half, put your thumb and index finger in the corners of the square folds on one side, and do the same with your other thumb and index finger on the other side.

3. Close the fortune teller by pinching your fingers and thumbs together in the centre, so all you can see are the squares with the coloured dots. Ask someone to choose a colour. Spell out the colour (or word), and with each letter alternate between opening the fortune teller one way (up and down) and then the other (left and right). If you used numbers, count from one to that number.

4. Stop and keep the fortune teller open on the last letter or number that you say out loud. Four numbers on the centre flaps should be visible. Ask someone to choose a number. Count to that number, again opening the fortune teller one way (up and down) and then the other (left and right).

5. Stop and keep the fortune teller open when you reach the chosen number. Lift the flap and read out the fortune, forfeit, joke or whatever you chose to write.

. . . MY PHONE

Obviously the main thing here is to hand them your phone to watch videos, right? Well, that's what I do anyway. My kids love swiping through old photos and videos on my phone, although we have to be careful what they see. (I'm thinking here of pictures of potential gifts, so take your mind out of the gutter!) And of course they also love a bit of YouTube Kids from time to time as well. But there are some other things we could use our phones for if you have these apps . . .

1. DOODLE
You can turn your phone into a notepad for them to draw on. It also means you can play some of the pen and paper games from pages 214–215.

2. PLAYGROUND BUDDY
This app is brilliant as it means you can find a playground near you! So grab your phone, follow the map and find a park for them to run around in if you can.

3. SKYVIEW
This is brilliant if it's night-time. Hold your phone up to the night sky, open this app and it will tell you where the stars are. It also tracks the ISS (International Space Station) and shows you the constellations. It works from both outside and inside the house.

4. KINDLE AND AUDIBLE
Both of these are great apps for stories. You can download books to your phone for the kids to listen to on journeys or if they're unable to go anywhere.

5. CBEEBIES GO EXPLORE
The BBC do some brilliant children's games apps and they're always free.

6. DICE

Download this app so you can play the dice games on pages 228–229.

7. CALCULATOR

You'd be surprised how long the calculator on your phone can keep a little one busy for. Don't forget to show them **5318008** upside down: **BOOBIES!** Hehe!

8. PODCASTS

If you have a podcast player on your phone, search out the child/family-focused ones to listen to. There are a wide range of subjects now, so just find one your child might like based on their interests. There are some suggestions on page 51.

9. GEOCACHING OR POKÉMON GO

As described on page 65, these apps are great if you fancy a walk. Or go to the website for Wiki Places for Kids, which shows you a map of places to go nearby, or just explore maps digitally.

10. YAKLIBS

This is a great game for getting kids to read and write as it makes up silly stories from random words it prompts you to type in.

11. CAMERA

If you leave the Guided Access function on, you can give your phone to your child and challenge them to take photos of things: 'Can you take a photo of something orange/soft/funny/beautiful/spiky?' (and so on). For older ones, make it a bit harder by asking them to find something that fits two adjectives; for example, 'Can you take a photo of something that's orange and beautiful?'

. . . MY WALLET

If I've let the house in a hurry and my phone is running out of battery, I'm sometimes only left with my wallet or purse as a form of entertainment. You might think that this means I have nothing to keep my little nose-miners occupied for five minutes, but actually no – that's not the case! There's plenty in there that can keep little hands busy for a wee while . . .

THINGS TO DO WITH COINS:

1. **MATCH THEM UP.**

2. **PUT THEM IN SIZE ORDER.**

3. **PUT THEM IN VALUE ORDER.**

4. **MAKE A TOWER.**

5. **PLAY HEADS OR TAILS.**

6. **SHOVE THEM ACROSS A TABLE** and see if you can make them stop with a bit overhanging but without falling off the table.

7. **SPIN THEM** – both spin a coin and see whose coin spins the longest.

8. **PLAY HIGHER OR LOWER.** Jiggle the coins in your hands and pick one without looking. They have to predict if it'll be higher or lower than the last coin. Can they empty your hands by guessing them all correctly?

9. **PLAY SHOPS.** Tell them to think of an item they want. Say how much it is. Can they get the right amount together from all the coins? If there is change, how much would it be?

10. **PLAY MONEY BOULES.** Make one coin the jack on a floor or table. You have two other coins each. Take it in turns to shove them or roll them along the surface trying to get yours as close to the jack coin as possible. The winner is the one with the nearest coin to the jack.

THINGS TO DO WITH CREDIT CARDS:

1. **MAKE LITTLE TUNNELS FOR COIN 'CARS' TO ROLL THROUGH.**

2. **BUILD A PYRAMID**

3. **USE THEM AS A SPRINGBOARD FOR COIN 'DIVERS'** by gripping them tightly to the edge of a solid surface, putting a coin on the edge hanging over the side and then pinging them upward. Give each 'dive' a score out of ten or see if the other person can catch the diving coin.

THINGS TO DO WITH OLD RECEIPTS:

1. **USE ANY RECEIPTS AS PAPER.** Often when out and about you can borrow a pen from somewhere for any of the pen and paper games on pages 214–215.

2. **USE RECEIPTS AS SMALL BALLS AND PLAY BLOW FOOTBALL**, or create a small penalty shootout on a table by using two coins as goalposts and your finger as the kicker or goalkeeper.

3. **USE THEM AS THE DIVER INSTEAD OF A COIN IN THE CREDIT CARD GAME** above if you're worried a flicked coin might do some damage where you are.

4. **PUT YOUR WALLET OR PURSE ON THE FLOOR BETWEEN YOU.** Each put a receipt over your mouth while looking up at the sky so it's balanced there. You both have to blow your receipt up into the air and the one that lands the closest to the wallet wins. Or you could also play 'Who can keep theirs in the air the longest without touching it?' but you need to make sure you start at the same height and clap as the signal to go.

. . . A DICE

OK, so why on earth would I be out and about with only a dice? Ha! I hear ya. Now I don't know about you, but I find it genuinely astounding the stuff that I find in my pockets or at the bottom of my handbag that my kids have handed me and I've put there for safe keeping. However, even if you don't have a dice at the bottom of your bag, you can easily download the *Dice Roll* app for free on your phone and then – **BOOM!** – you've got some games!

The best way to play dice games when out and about? Have one in a small plastic see-through container. Then you can shake the container to roll it without it flying under a neighbouring table or into the footwell of your car.

1. ROLL AND GO

Assign a movement to a number. For example, if someone rolls a three you have to touch your nose, or if someone rolls a six you have to stand up. Then take it in turns to roll, and if the number comes up you have to do the action as quickly as possible. First one to do it wins. Maybe add up points and first to get to ten is the champion! If you want to make it trickier assign moves to more numbers. Perhaps all six!

2. PICK A NUMBER

Choose a number between one and six and say it aloud. Count how many rolls you have to do before you get it. Let the next player do the same. Can they beat you with fewer rolls?

3. PLAY ODDS OR EVENS

Call it before you roll, like heads or tails. How many can you get right in a row?

4. PLAY NUMBER I SPY

Roll the dice, and whatever number comes up it is the amount of an item you need to spot. So if you roll a four you might have to try to find four ducks in a pond, or four spots on someone's dress. The only rule is it can't be the same item twice. First one to shout something out wins and gets to roll the dice next.

5. HIGHER OR LOWER

One person rolls once, then whatever number they get they have to predict if the next roll will be higher or lower. Depending on your kids, you can either make the rule that rolling the same again just means they have another go, or you can say the old Bruce Forsyth catchphrase 'Nothing for a pair in this game' and they lose. Everyone takes a turn rolling and predicting. The winner is the one who does the most rolls predicting if it'll be higher or lower correctly.

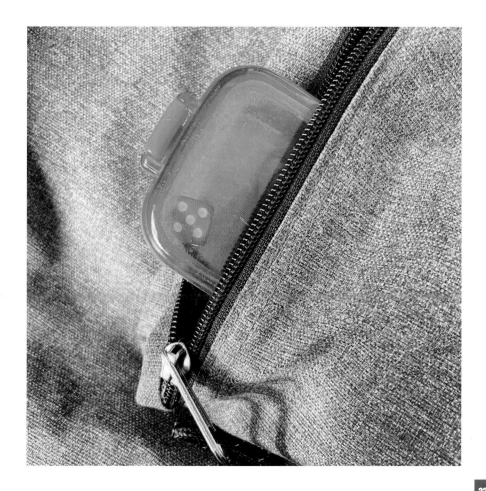

Making a mess by playing games with sachets and serviettes is a perfect way to teach our little ones about cleaning up after ourselves when out and about. Now if only there was a game that could teach them to do this at home too . . . !

. . . SERVIETTES AND SUGAR SACHETS IN A RESTAURANT

Such is life that sometimes you plonk yourselves down on at a table in a cafe and quickly realize that you have nothing on you, and your small humans are causing instant havoc. Unless they are immediately occupied, you will find them attempting to lick the salt or catapult knives and forks perilously close to neighbouring diners. But if there are serviettes and maybe some sachets at the table, then you can have yourselves a little game time, which might just keep them busy long enough for the menus to arrive.

1 Play **I SPY,** but instead of saying the letter the thing starts with, spell it out using the sachets.

2 If there are enough, **CREATE A RACETRACK** on the table and use another sachet as your car. Try to flick it round the track using one finger without hitting the sides.

3 Ask to borrow a pen and use the serviette as paper for the **PEN AND PAPER GAMES** on pages 214–215.

4 Play **NUMBER THIEF** with the numbers written on ten bits of a torn-up serviette (see page 183).

5 Empty the pot that the sugar sachets are stored in. Take a sachet each. Put it on the edge of the table so one end is overhanging. Using your hand, try to **FLIP THE SACHET INTO THE POT** in one go.

. . . A BALL

Again, why would I have a ball but nothing else? Well, you might not **THINK** you have a ball, but if you – or anyone you are with – is wearing socks, you have a ball! Oh yes, there have been so many times where we've used balled-up socks to play and entertain ourselves. Here are some of our games:

1. HOOPS

One person creates a hoop out of their arms linked in front of them. The other person stands in front of the hoop with the ball. They have to throw it through the hoop – if it goes in, then they take a step backwards and shoot again. Each time they score they take a step back. See how many steps back they can go before they miss, then swap over and the other person has a turn to see if they can do more steps by shooting more hoops in a row! The person who is the hoop must not move!!

2. THE RADIATOR GAME

In my parents' house they have a radiator against the wall in the lounge. Often, of an evening, we could take our socks off, ball them up and throw them to try to get them to land perfectly on top of the radiator or between the radiator to the wall – something silly that always made us laugh. I showed Ewan the other day and he started aiming his socks at all kinds of things!

3. PIGGY IN THE MIDDLE

You need three people or more for this game. One person is the 'piggy' and they must attempt to intercept the ball between the other players who throw it between them. As soon as they are successful, the person who threw the ball they intercepted becomes the piggy.

4. DROP IT

As many players as you like pass the ball to each other in a circle. If a player drops it, they must drop down on to one knee for their next go. If they then catch the ball on their next turn, they may return to standing on two legs – but if they drop it again, they must then kneel on both knees. If they continue to drop the ball, they have to move to a sitting position and then put one hand behind their back that they can't use. If they drop it yet again, that player is out. Players keep changing positions based on whether they've caught or dropped the ball as they continue to throw the ball round the circle.

5. DODGEBALL

Decide on a specific play space. An even number of players stand on opposite sides of the play space. Decide on an imaginary line that divides the two teams that each cannot cross. You must try to hit the opposition with a ball (or lots of balled-up socks!) from the waist down. If you are hit, you must leave the play space. If a player catches a ball without it bouncing from the opposition's throw, they are allowed to bring a player who is out back into the game. The winning team is the first team to get everyone on the opposition team out.

STOP, DROP
AND PLAY

I am writing these final words to you from my car as I sit waiting for Florence to finish her Monday night gymnastics class, laptop balanced precariously between my knees and the steering wheel. It is not lost on me just how much I am in keeping with the **ON THE GO** title of this book right now! But that's everyday life with a busy family, isn't it? It doesn't matter if there are two of you or twenty of you; when it comes to the ones we love the most, we will do whatever it takes to make them happy. And, for those with young children, that often means getting creative to fit everything in, whether that means wedging in homework as we scoff down breakfast, doing a work call as we dash home from the nursery drop-off, or nipping to the shops before we head out on that long overdue run we promised ourselves.

Often it can seem that making time for **FUN** is very low on the list of priorities. I get it. Sometimes our fast-paced world feels too relentless to make time for play. But I hope that these pages of games, both new and old, have helped you to see that we can still fit it in around our hectic lives. And I very much believe we should!

Being able to find joy and fun and laughter in the everyday is, for me, the secret to happiness. When I stop for a moment and take five minutes to play with the two little humans I have created, I feel better about myself. I connect with them, and I find out things that I might otherwise not have noticed. It is a crucial part of our relationship.

But, more recently, I've found that play can do this with our own parents too or those from the generations above us. We can reminisce through play. How often do our fondest memories include games and silly competitions we made up with family or friends? Ask people you know about their memories of childhood and I'll bet there's a game in there somewhere. Despite being buried under life admin, emails and to-do lists, playfulness survives in all of us.

Let me tell you a little story about why I think it is so important. We took Ewan to a care home to meet his great-grandmother a few years ago. She had

Lots of the games in this book are my own family games, passed down through generations. You can download blank games pages from my website fiveminutemum.com so that you too can write the rules and equipment needed for your own games, to add to those in this book. I hope this book helps to initiate conversations about play with your friends and family from days gone by and helps you to create your very own bible of play, to be passed on like a wonderful heirloom!

dementia and was in the final months of her life, so the mood was understandably rather subdued. But after a few minutes he put the toy car he was clutching on her lap and then drove it around her chair. Her demeanour instantly changed. She smiled and said, 'Whoosh,' as she bent over to push the little car back to him along the floor. His glee at finding someone to play with lit up his two-year-old face. Just a little game? Yes, maybe, but also precious final memories.

So never underestimate the power of play. Harness it when you can. Gather together those you love most and initiate a game. Squeeze it in during car journeys and queues. It doesn't matter how old you are, or how important or serious you might feel you have become. If you're planting your face into a mound of flour to retrieve a matchstick, or throwing balled-up socks across a room to try to score the final point, then you're being your best self!

And, if in doubt, take your lead from the children. Because play comes naturally to them. Give them this book and let them choose something to set up, then put down the laptop or washing-up gloves and join in with them. I promise it won't be a wasted five minutes. Utilize the time while you're **ON THE GO** if you must, but don't forget that sometimes there is nothing better than stopping and remembering what it is to just **PLAY**!

ACKNOWLEDGEMENTS

The first people to thank here are obviously the awesome 'crew' in this book.

Firstly, my ever-incredible mum and dad, Jennie and Cliff, and my awesome father-in-law (Grandad!), Willie, and his wife, Jeanette. We moved so we could be nearer to each other and, boy, is it the best decision we made.

Next up are my three best friends and their families. These girls are my chosen ones. The kids call them aunties and I don't know where I would be without their ongoing, constant, unconditional love and support. They are the BEST: Nic and Seni, and their two children, Amelie and Grace; Sneha and Ben; Danielle and Ben, and their nephew Felix, and his parents, Dominic and Nadia. I can't thank you enough . . . Let's do it again soon – I'll call the pizza van!

I would also like to thank everyone at Penguin Random House who has had something to do with my books but especially: Ruth Knowles, Ben Hughes, Lol Johnson, Abbie Fisk, Nikki Dupin and her team at Nic&Lou, especially Laura Bayliss – all your skills and talents are what truly make this book a team effort. Special thanks go to Pippa Shaw for her excellent editorial notes and fantastic suggestions, and to Wendy Shakespeare, whose patience and knowledge has made the complicated editing process a constant delight.

Enormous thanks to Katie Kirby – I've been a fan of hers for years and LOVED her pics popping up daily on Facebook to restore my sanity during early motherhood. So the fact she has drawn me and my family is right up there. #LifeGoals. Thanks so much for squeezing me in, Katie, and for adding your wonderful humour to my book.

Huge gratitude to Becky Fox, Emma Marshall, Sydney Piercey and Myriam Sandler for inspiring me and allowing me to add their brilliant tips to this book.

Big hugs also to my agent, Lauren. You are about to read my books from a very different perspective! I am wishing you all the luck in the world.

And, finally, my people – the ones who have to put up with me all the time, throughout three books and five years of doing this, and who have never once said, 'Oh really! Not again?' My husband, Kenny: thank you, thank you, thank you for everything you do. And it is A LOT! And to Ewan and Florence. Like I said at the very beginning of my first book, I did it all for you.

INDEX

A

Action Box 177–81
After Eights Game 85
Audible 221
audiobooks 51, 221

B

ball games 232–3
balloons 72
 Action Box 177–81
 Balloon Relay 74
 Drop and Pop 73
 Musical Balloons 73
 Water Balloon Hunt 123
bath time 161
bingo: Bingo Limbo 79
 Car Bingo 57
 video chats 127
binoculars 65
board games: video chats
 125
books: audiobooks 51, 221
 car journeys 53
 on video chats 129
boredom 8
boules: Golf-Ball Boules 115
 Money Boules 225
Box of Tricks 168–9
 Action Box 177–81
 Challenge Box 195–9
 Creative Play Box 171–5
 Let's Learn Box 183–7
 Sensory Box 189–93

bubble mix 12
 for funerals 137
Buckaroo 159
Budding Artists 129

C

calculators 223
cameras 223
Car Bingo 57
The Car Hunt 63
car journeys 47–57, 64
car seats 54–5
CBeebies Go Explore 221
Cereal Box Game 77
ceremonies
 see formal occasions
Challenge Box 195–9
The Checklist Hunt 61
The Chocolate Game 80–81
Chopstick Maltesers 83
coins 225
The Collection Hunt 61
colouring books: car
 journeys 53
 poorly parents 161
compasses 65
Compound Game 203
Creative Play Box 171–5
credit cards 227

D

Dance-Off 127
dice games 228–9

Challenge Box 195–9
 on phones 223
 The Chocolate Game
 80–81
Do You Know? 129
Doctors and Nurses 157
Dodgeball 233
doodling: on phones 221
Dots and Squares 214
Doughnut Limbo 83
Drop and Pop 73
Drop It 232–3
Duck Duck Goose 107

F

family parties
 see get-togethers
*50 Fantastic Ideas for Forest
 School* (Barnes) 65
final and first box 147
finding games: video chats
 125
five-year-olds: Tat Bags
 21–3
Flip Cup 117–19
flotation devices 33
The Flour Game 96–7
foam shapes 41
food: party games 80–85
 theme parks 66
formal occasions 133
 funerals 137
 weddings 134–5

fortune tellers 197, 215, 216–19
four-year-olds: Tat Bags 19
friends and family get togethers *see* get-togethers
Frisbee Capture 164
funerals 137

G

The Generation Game 129
geocaching 65, 223
get-togethers 71
  games for parties 73–9
  hunger games 80–85
  indoor games 87–103
  outdoor games 105–115
  video-chat games 125–9
  water games for hot days 117–23
Golden Rule 8–9
Golf-Ball Boules 115
Grids and Battleships 215
Guess That Song 57
Guess That Toy 127

H

hair bobbles 12
hand gel 13
Hangman 214
headphones: car journeys 53
high-chair games 150–51

Higher or Lower: with coins 225
  with dice 229
holidays 30–33
Hoops 232
Hopscotch 113, 185
hospital stays 162–3
  vomit bowl games 164–5
hotels: theme parks 67
hunger games 80–85
hunts: The Car Hunt 63
  The Checklist Hunt 61
  The Collection Hunt 61
  The Ribbon Hunt 63
  The Traffic Hunt 61–3
  Water Balloon Hunt 123

I

I Spy 66, 203
  Number I Spy 228
  using sugar sachets 231
I Went to the Shops and I Bought 66, 203
illness: hospital stays 162–5
  poorly parents 157–61
indoor games 87–103

J

Jelly-Bean Hunt 85
jigsaw puzzles: poorly parents 160, 161

K

Kindle 221
kit list 11–13
Kitchen Tennis 89
knickers 12

L

Lace Race 103
Ladders 109
Let's Learn Box 183–7
letters: Let's Learn Box 183–7
limbo: Bingo Limbo 79
  Doughnut Limbo 83
Link Stories 57, 66
lollipops 12
  in cars 51
  on planes 32
  for weddings 134
Lorry Count 57
Lotto 215

M

Magic Traffic Lights 57
Maltesers: Chopstick Maltesers 83
memory books: moving house 45
mobile-phone games 221–3
Money Boules 225
Movie Day 159
moving house 143–5

high-chair games 150–51
moving day 146–9
packaging games 152–3
Musical Balloons 73
Musical Bumps 159
Musical Statues 159

N

napkins 231
newborns: car travel 54
night-time car journeys 47
Noughts and Crosses 214
  see also Tic-Tac-Toe
Number I Spy 228
Number Thief 183, 231
numbers: Let's Learn Box
  183–7

O

Odds or Evens 197, 228
Olympic Wall Squash 94–5
one-year-olds: Tat Bags 17
out and about near home
  59
outdoor games 105–115
  water games for hot days
  117–23

P

packaging games 152–3
packing cubes 32
pants 12

Paper Shuffle 91
paracetamol 12
parents: poorly 157–61
party games 73–9
  with food 80–85
pen and paper games
  214–17
  using receipts 227
  using serviettes 231
pens 12
phone games 221–3
Pick a Number 228
Piggy in the Middle 232
planes 32, 37–43
plasters 11
play dough 26–7
  Creative Play Box 171–5
  on planes 32, 39
Playground Buddy 55, 221
podcasts 223
Pokémon GO 65, 223
poorly parents 157–61
Posting Pot 164
potty 51
puppet shows: video chats
  127
purses 225–7

R

The Radiator Game 232
Raspberry Face 214
reading: on video chats 129
receipts 227
restaurants: serviettes and

sugar sachets 231
The Revolving Door 213
The Ribbon Hunt 63
Rock, Paper, Scissors 203
Roll and Go 228
rubbish bin: car journeys 53
rucksacks 11
  train journeys 45

S

safety 3
  car safety 54–5
  out and about safety 59
The Salon 157
Salt Dough Tic-Tac-Toe
  99–101
The Scarecrows' Wedding
  (Donaldson) 135
schools: moving house 145,
  154–5
Sensory Box 189–93
serviettes 231
Sick Box: car journeys
  49–51
sickness see illness
Silly Soup 187
Simon Says 66, 203
six-year-olds: Tat Bags 21–3
six-plus Tat Bags 25
SkyView 221
Sleeping Lions 159
Snack Boxes 13
  car journeys 51
  holidays 32

Snack Tombola 41
socks 12
    as balls 232
Splat 121
squash: Olympic Wall
    Squash 94–5
Steal the Keys 159
storage-pouch washing
    line 41
stories: Link Stories 57, 66
    Yaklibs 223
sugar sachets 231

T
tablets: car journeys 53
Tat Bags 14–27
    car journeys 53
    at funerals 137
    holidays 32
    hospital stays 163, 164
    on planes 39, 43
Tea Cups 111
tennis: Kitchen Tennis 89
theme parks 66–7
three-year-olds: Tat Bags 19
Tic-Tac-Toe: Salt Dough
    Tic-Tac-Toe 99–101
    see also Noughts and
        Crosses
Tights Relay 75
Tissue Toss 164
toddlers: Sensory Box
    189–93
tombola: Toy Tombola 41,

127, 183–4
towels 12
Toy Tombola 41, 183–4
    video chats 127
The Traffic Hunt 61–3
traffic lights 57
trains 45
travel potty 51
treasure hunts see
    geocaching; hunts
tricky times 141
    hospital stays 162–5
    moving house 143–53
    new school 154–5
    poorly parents 157–61
Two Truths, One Lie 207
    211
two-year-olds: Tat Bags 17

U
underwear 12

V
video-chat games 125–9
vomit bowl games 164–5

W
Waft It 93
walks 61–5
Wall Squash 94–5
wallets 225–7
washing line 41, 184

Water Balloon Hunt 123
water games 117–23
Waze 55
weddings 134–5
We're Going on a Bear
    Hunt (Rosen and
    Oxenbury) 65, 129
wet wipes 12
What's in the Bowl? 165
Who's Hiding? 164
Wiki Places for Kids 223
wipes 12
Would You Rather . . . ? 66,
    129, 204–5
wrecking ball 184

Y
Yaklibs 223

Z
zip bags 11

5 minutes' peace